Title: Qabalah - The Book of Enoch -
The Book of Watchers

Editor: Steven Ashe

Category: Religion & Spirituality

Publisher: Glastonbury Books 2008

Edition: First Hardback Edition

http://www.glastonburybooks.com

Qabalah
THE BOOK
OF ENOCH
The Book of Watchers

Steven Ashe
Glastonbury Books 2008

ISBN: 978-0-9556932-0-5

Introduction

By

Steven Ashe

The Book of Enoch was not as highly regarded amongst students of the Judaic Talmudic tradition as amongst Christian scholars. The author of the Apocryphal Christian text known as The Book of Jubilees certainly used Enoch as a source and inspiration.

During the early Dark Ages, the work was lost to literary scholars apart from fragments preserved in the writings of Syncellus and has been reconstructed from later Greek and Ethiopic sources. It was not until 1773, when the famous Scottish explorer James Bruce retrieved three seperate manuscripts from Etheopea (then Abyssinia) which found their way into the collections of the Bodleian Library, the Royal Library of France and his own personal collection of papers, that scholastic scrutiny could be brought to bear upon this work in its entirety. It was from these sources that Professor Laurence, Archbishop of Cashel compiled his English translation of 1821.

The Old Testament prophet Enoch, the son of Jared (Genesis v. 18) is described as such in in the apocryphal Christian text known as the Epistle of Barnabus (chapter 4, verse three) and also in the New Testament Letter of Jude (verse 14).

Enoch is described in Genesis (verse 21 - 24) as having *walked with God* and having been taken by God unto Heaven:

"And Enoch lived sixty and five years, and begat Methuselah: And Enoch walked with God after he begat Methuselah three hundred years, and begat sons and daughters: And all the days of Enoch were three hundred sixty and five years: And Enoch walked with God: and he was not; for God took him."

(Genesis 21 -24 King James Version)

The opening text of chapter twelve of The Book of Enoch describes the prophets dealings with the Angels known as Watchers:

"Before these things Enoch was hidden, and no one of the children of men knew where he was hidden, and where he abode, and what had become of him. And his activities had to do with the Watchers, and his days were with the holy ones."

The divine knowledge which Enoch brought to Earth from Heaven is parallel to the achievements of Prometheus in Greek myth. In the Judaic tradition he is known as the father of Astronomy, Arithmetic and the alphabet. Islamic tradition accords him the honour of the invention of both literature and sewing, but he is mentioned in the Qu'ran only once by the name of Edris, the learned (Surah 19 verse 57), where he is described as a prophet. The Qur'anic scholar Beidawi ascribes the authorship of thirty divinely inspired books to Enoch.

After the judgment passed upon the Fallen Angels by the their heavenly father, the prophet is asked to author a petition for the Angels requesting mercy and forgiveness. For this reason, Enoch is regarded by occultists as an intermediary between the Angelic realm and the Heavenly and Earthly realms. Diverse occult methods of communication with the Angelic forms have been attempted by esoteric adventurers such as John Dee and Edward Kelley since 1582 onwards. Kelly, scryer and visionary under Dee's patronage of operations of mystical inquiry, claimed to have knowledge of the language of the Angelic realm. His visions as recorded by Dee acting as Scribe, employing a skrying crystal and pools of black ink, describe mystical forms tapping out sequences of letters upon crossword-like tables.

The occultist Macgregor Mathers expanded the Dee material into a unique system particularly tailored to his Order of the Golden Dawn material; influencing Aleister Crowley who, with the English poet Victor Neuberg, performed an incredible series of rites based upon methods of *skrying in the spirit vision* employing Dee and Kelly's Enochian Calls in the Algerian desert in the early 1900s. Crowley published these experiences in his work 'The Vision and the Voice' reproduced in his journal The Equinox: full of highly imaginative symbolic imagery consonant with Crowley's interpretation of Hermetic-Qabalistic lore.

Mather's and Crowley's focus upon the word-square tables described by Kelley employ only four of the word–square tablets which are known as the Tablets of the Elemental Watchtowers. These are balanced and given a talismanic synthesis in a fifth table known as the Tablet of Union; each of the visionary experiences being accessed through inspiration via magical invocations or 'Calls'.

In his Liber Logaeth, Dee states: "I am therefore to instruct and inform you, according to your Doctrine delivered, which is contained in 49 Tables. In 49 voices, or callings: which are the Natural Keys to open those, not 49 but 48 (for one is not to be opened) Gates of Understanding, whereby you shall have knowledge to move every Gate..."

Also, Dee writes in the same work: "But you shall understand that these 19 Calls are the Calls, or entrances into the knowledge of the mystical Tables. Every Table containing one whole leaf, whereunto you need no other circumstances."

The Fallen Angels of The Book of Enoch begat beings known to Qabalists as 'The Nephilim' םילפנ and were described in the Old Testament thus:

"Now it came about, when men began to multiply on the face of the land, and daughters were born to them, that the sons of God saw that the daughters of men were beautiful; and they took wives for themselves, whomever they chose. Then the LORD said, "My Spirit shall not strive with man forever, because he also is flesh; nevertheless his days shall be one hundred and twenty years." The Nephilim were on the earth in those days, and also afterward, when the sons of God came in to the daughters of men, and they bore children to them.

Those were the mighty men who were of old, men of renown. "

(Genesis, chapter 6, verses 1 - 4)

The epistle of Jude from the Christian New Testament has the following to say:

"The angels too, who did not keep to their own domain but deserted their proper dwelling, he has kept in eternal chains, in gloom, for the judgment of the great day. Likewise, Sodom, Gomorrah, and the surrounding towns, which, in the same manner as they, indulged in sexual promiscuity and practiced unnatural vice, serve as an example by undergoing a punishment of eternal fire".

In Aramaic lore, the phrase Nephila denoted the stellar constellation of Orion. The term Nephilim therefore denotes Orion's descendents, a race of demi-gods perhaps indicative of the gods of the epoch of pre - Jehovah worship which the Semitic shepherd tribes may have embraced during their wanderings beneath the open skies of the Middle East.

Such entities may have become demonised as the Semitic culture embraced monotheism through the worship of Jehovah. This is certainly consistent with the treatment of the gods of elder cultures whose worship has been succeeded by usurping deities. The demons of one culture are often the gods of an elder culture.

Whatever the origin of the Fallen Angels and their spawn, reports of spiritual beings bequeathing the knowledge of the

Arts and Sciences to mankind are common to the mythologies of every continent. In the spiritual tradition of the Qabalah, these entities are often regarded as malefic. Their leader being transformed into the great Satan, enemy of God. In the Islamic tradition, the leader of the fallen angels is seen to be quite the opposite; that is as the enemy of Man, having refused to bow down to Adam at the behest of Allah because of his previous oath to the Creator not to worship any being other than the Lord.

The Book of Enoch may not form a part of the canon of official scriptures of the Western Christian tradition, but it does rank amongst the inspirational sources of the early Church Fathers and was certainly a popular text available for scrutiny by the prophet Jesus and his disciples. The Ethiopian Orthodox Church still cherishes the work as a text of incisive religious inspiration truth and scholars of Western esoteric lore continue to revere its mythic elements as indicative of deep symbolic significance in their attempts to decode the mysteries of the visionary Qabalah.

Steven Ashe, Glastonbury (2008)

The Book of Enoch

1 The words of the blessing of Enoch, wherewith he blessed the elect and righteous, who will be 2 living in the day of tribulation, when all the wicked and godless are to be removed. And he took up his parable and said, "Enoch a righteous man, whose eyes were opened by God, saw the vision of the Holy One in the heavens, which the angels showed me, and from them I heard everything, and from them I understood as I saw, but not for this generation, but for a remote one which is 3 for to come. Concerning the elect I said, and took up my parable concerning them: The Holy Great One will come forth from His dwelling, 4 And the eternal God will tread upon the earth, (even) on Mount Sinai, [And appear from His camp] And appear in the strength of His might from the heaven of heaven. 5 And all shall be smitten with fear, And the Watchers shall quake, And great fear and trembling shall seize them unto the ends of the earth. 6 And the high mountains shall be shaken, And the high hills shall be made low, And shall melt like wax before the flame. And the earth shall be wholly rent in sunder, And all that is upon the earth shall perish, And there shall be a judgment upon all (men). But with the righteous He will make peace, And will protect the elect, And. mercy shall be upon them. And they shall all belong to God, And they shall be prospered, And they shall all be blessed. And He will help them all, And light shall appear unto them, And

He will make peace with them. 9 And behold! He cometh with ten thousands of His holy ones To execute judgment upon all, And to destroy all the ungodly: And to convict all flesh of all the works of their ungodliness which they have ungodly committed, And of all the hard things which ungodly sinners have spoken against Him.

2 1 Observe ye everything that takes place in the heaven, how they do not change their orbits, and the luminaries which are in the heaven, how they all rise and set in order each in its season, and transgress 2 not against their appointed order. Behold ye the earth, and give heed to the things which take place upon it from first to last, how steadfast they are how none of the things upon earth 3 change, but all the works of God appear to you. Behold the summer and the winter, how the whole earth is filled with water, and clouds and dew and rain lie upon it.

3 Observe and see how (in the winter) all the trees seem as though they had withered and shed all their leaves, except fourteen trees, which do not lose their foliage but retain the old foliage from two to three years till the new comes.

4 And again, observe ye the days of summer how the sun is above the earth over against it. And you seek shade and shelter by reason of the heat of the sun, and the earth also burns with glowing heat, and so you cannot tread on the earth, or on a rock by reason of its heat.

5 1 Observe ye how the trees cover themselves with green leaves and bear fruit: wherefore give ye heed and know with regard to all His works, and recognize how He that liveth for ever hath made them so. 2 And all His works go on thus from year to year for ever, and all the tasks which they accomplish for Him, and their tasks change not, but according as God hath ordained so is it done. 3 And behold how the sea and the rivers in like manner accomplish and change not their tasks from His commandments. 4 But ye -- ye have not been steadfast, nor done the commandments of the Lord, But ye have turned away and spoken proud and hard words With your impure mouths against His greatness. Oh, ye hard-hearted, ye shall find no peace. 5 Therefore shall ye execrate your days, And the years of your life shall perish, And the years of your destruction shall be multiplied in eternal execration, And ye shall find no mercy. 6a In those days ye shall make your names an eternal execration unto all the righteous, b And by you shall all who curse, curse, And all the sinners and godless shall imprecate by you, 7c And for you the godless there shall be a curse. 6d And all the... shall rejoice, e And there shall be forgiveness of sins, And every mercy and peace and forbearance: There shall be salvation unto them, a goodly light. And for all of you sinners there shall be no salvation, But on you all shall abide a curse. 7a But for the elect there shall be light and joy and peace, And they shall inherit the earth. 8 And then there shall be bestowed upon the elect wisdom, And they shall all live and never again sin, Either through ungodliness or through pride: But they who are wise shall be humble. 9 And they shall not again transgress, Nor shall they sin all the days of their life, Nor shall they die of (the divine) anger or wrath, But they shall complete the number of the days of their life. And their lives shall be increased in peace, And the years of their joy shall be multiplied, In eternal gladness and peace, all the days of their life.

6 1 And it came to pass when the children of men had multiplied that in those days were born unto 2 them beautiful and comely daughters. And the angels, the children of the heaven, saw and lusted after them, and said to one another: 'Come, let us choose us wives from among the children of men 3 and beget us children.' And Semjaza, who

was their leader, said unto them: 'I fear ye will not 4 indeed agree to do this deed, and I alone shall have to pay the penalty of a great sin.' And they all answered him and said: 'Let us all swear an oath, and all bind ourselves by mutual imprecations 5 not to abandon this plan but to do this thing.' Then sworn they all together bound themselves 6 by mutual imprecations upon it. And they were in all two hundred; who descended in the days of Jared on the summit of Mount Hermon, and they called it Mount Hermon, because they had sworn 7 and bound themselves by mutual imprecations upon it. And these are the names of their leaders: Samiazaz, their leader, Arakiba, Rameel, Kokabiel, Tamiel, Ramiel, Danel, Ezeqeel, Baraqijal, 8 Asael, Armaros, Batarel, Ananel, Zaqiel, Samsapeel, Satarel, Turel, Jomjael, Sariel. These are their chiefs of tens.

7 1 And all the others together with them took unto themselves wives, and each chose for himself one, and they began to go in unto them and to defile themselves with them, and they taught them charms 2 and enchantments, and the cutting of roots, and made them acquainted with plants. And they 3 became pregnant, and they bare great giants, whose height was three thousand ells: Who consumed 4 all the acquisitions of men. And when men could no longer sustain them, the giants turned against 5 them and devoured mankind. And they began to sin against birds, and beasts, and reptiles, and 6 fish, and to devour one another's flesh, and drink the blood. Then the earth laid accusation against the lawless ones.

8 1 And Azazel taught men to make swords, and knives, and shields, and breastplates, and made known to them the metals (of the earth) and the art of working them, and bracelets, and ornaments, and the use of antimony, and the beautifying of the eyelids, and all kinds of costly stones, and

all 2 colouring tinctures. And there arose much godlessness, and they committed fornication, and they 3 were led astray, and became corrupt in all their ways. Semjaza taught enchantments, and rootcuttings, Armaros the resolving of enchantments, Baraqijal (taught) astrology, Kokabel the constellations, Ezeqeel the knowledge of the clouds, (Araqiel the signs of the earth, Shamsiel the signs 4 of the sun), and Sariel the course of the moon. And as men perished, they cried, and their cry went up to heaven...

9 1 And then Michael, Uriel, Raphael, and Gabriel looked down from heaven and saw much blood being 2 shed upon the earth, and all lawlessness being wrought upon the earth. And they said one to another: 'The earth made without inhabitant cries the voice of their cryings up to the gates of heaven. 3 And now to you, the holy ones of heaven, the souls of men make their suit, saying, Bring our cause 4 before the Most High.' And they said to the Lord of the ages: ' Lord of lords, God of gods, King of kings, (and God of the ages); the throne of Thy glory (standeth) unto all the generations of the 5 ages, and Thy name holy and glorious and blessed unto all the ages! Thou hast made all things, and power over all things hast Thou: and all things are naked and open in Thy sight, and Thou seest all 6 things, and nothing can hide itself from Thee. Thou seest what Azazel hath done, who hath taught all unrighteousness on earth and revealed the eternal secrets which were (preserved) in heaven, which men were striving to learn: And Semjaza, to whom Thou hast given authority to bear rule over 8 his associates. And they have gone to the daughters of men upon the earth, and have slept with the 9 women, and have defiled themselves, and revealed to them all kinds of sins. And the women have 10 borne giants, and the whole earth has thereby been filled with blood and unrighteousness. And now, behold, the souls of those who have died are crying and making their suit to the gates of heaven, and their lamentations have ascended: and cannot cease because of the lawless deeds which are 11 wrought on the earth. And Thou knowest all things before they come to pass, and Thou seest these things and Thou dost suffer them, and Thou dost not say to us what we are to do to them in regard to these.'

10 1 Then said the Most High, the Holy and Great One spake, and sent Uriel to the son of Lamech, 2 and said to him: ('Go to Noah and) tell him in my name " Hide thyself!" and reveal to him the end that is approaching: that the whole earth will be destroyed, and a deluge is about to come 3 upon the whole earth, and will destroy all that is on it. And now instruct him that he may escape 4 and his seed may be preserved for all the generations of the world.' And again the Lord said to Raphael: 'Bind Azazel hand and foot, and cast him into the darkness: and make an opening 5 in the desert, which is in Dudael, and cast him therein. And place upon him rough and jagged rocks, and cover him with darkness, and let him abide there for ever, and cover his face that he may 6, 7 not see light. And on the day of the great judgement he shall be cast into the fire. And heal the earth which the angels have corrupted, and proclaim the healing of the earth, that they may heal the plague, and that all the children of men may not perish through all the secret things that the 8 Watchers have disclosed and have taught their sons. And the whole earth has been corrupted 9 through the works that were taught by Azazel: to him ascribe all sin.' And to Gabriel said the Lord: 'Proceed against the bastards and the reprobates, and against the children of fornication: and destroy [the children of fornication and] the children of the Watchers from amongst men: [and cause them to go forth]: send them one against the other that they may destroy each other in 10 battle: for length of days shall they not have. And no request that they (i.e. their fathers) make of thee shall be granted unto their fathers on their behalf; for they hope to live an eternal life, and 11 that each one of them will live five hundred years.' And the Lord said unto Michael: 'Go, bind Semjaza and his associates who have united themselves with women so as to have defiled themselves 12 with them in all their uncleanness. And when their sons have slain one another, and they have seen the destruction of their beloved ones, bind them fast for seventy generations in the valleys of the earth, till the day of their judgement and of their consummation, till the judgement that is 13 for ever and ever is consummated. In those days they shall be led off to the abyss of fire: (and) 14 to the torment and the prison in which they shall be confined for ever. And whosoever shall be condemned and destroyed will from thenceforth be bound together with them to the end of all 15 generations. And destroy all the spirits of the reprobate and the children of the Watchers, because 16 they have wronged mankind. Destroy all wrong from the face of the earth and let every evil work come to an end: and let the plant of righteousness and truth appear: and it shall prove a blessing; the works of righteousness and truth shall be planted in truth and joy for evermore. 17 And then shall all the righteous escape, And shall live till they beget thousands of children, And all the days of their youth and their old age Shall they complete in peace. 18 And then shall the whole earth be tilled in righteousness, and shall all be planted with trees and 19 be full of blessing. And all desirable trees shall be planted on it, and they shall plant vines on it: and the vine which they plant thereon shall yield wine in abundance, and as for all the seed which is sown thereon each measure (of it) shall bear a thousand, and each measure of olives shall yield 20 ten presses of oil. And cleanse thou the earth from all oppression, and from all unrighteousness, and from all sin, and from all godlessness: and all the uncleanness that is wrought upon the earth 21 destroy from off the earth. And all the children of men shall become righteous, and all nations 22 shall offer adoration and shall praise Me, and all shall worship Me. And the earth shall be cleansed from all defilement, and from all sin, and from all punishment, and from all torment, and I will never again send (them) upon it from generation to generation and for ever.

11 1 And in those days I will open the store chambers of blessing which are in the heaven, so as to send 2 them down upon the earth over the work and labour of the children of men. And truth and peace shall be associated together throughout all the days of the world and throughout all the generations of men.'

12 1 Before these things Enoch was hidden, and no one of the children of men knew where he was 2 hidden, and where he abode, and what had become of him. And his activities had to do with the Watchers, and his days were with the holy ones. 3 And I Enoch was blessing the Lord of majesty and the King of the ages, and lo! the Watchers 4 called me -- Enoch the scribe and said to me: 'Enoch, thou scribe of righteousness, go, declare to the Watchers of the heaven who have left the high heaven, the holy eternal place, and have defiled themselves with women, and have done as the children of earth do, and have taken unto themselves 5 wives : "Ye have wrought great destruction on the earth: And ye shall have no peace nor forgiveness 6 of sin: and inasmuch as they delight themselves in their children, The murder of their beloved ones shall they see, and over the destruction of their children shall they lament, and shall make supplication unto eternity, but mercy and peace shall ye not attain."

13 1 And Enoch went and said: 'Azazel, thou shalt have no peace: a severe sentence has gone forth 2 against thee to put thee in bonds: And thou shall not have toleration nor request granted to thee, because of the unrighteousness which thou hast taught, and because of all the works of godlessness 3 and unrighteousness and sin which thou hast shown to men.' Then I went and spoke to them all 4 together, and. they were all afraid, and fear and trembling seized them. And they besought me to draw up a petition for them that they might find forgiveness, and to read their petition in the presence 5 of the Lord of heaven. For from thenceforward they could not speak (with Him) nor lift up their 6 eyes to heaven for shame of their sins for which they had been condemned. Then I wrote out their petition, and the prayer till regard to their spirits and their deeds individually and in regard to their 7 requests that they should have forgiveness and length. And I went off and sat down at the waters of Dan, in the land of Dan, to the south of the west of Hermon: I read their petition till I fell 8 asleep. And behold a dream came to me, and visions fell down upon me, and I saw visions of chastisement, and a voice came bidding (me) to tell it to the sons of heaven, and reprimand them. 9 And when I awaked, I came unto them, and they were all sitting gathered together, weeping in 10 Abelsjail, which is between Lebanon and Seneser, with their faces covered. And I recounted before them all the visions which I had seen in sleep, and I began to speak the words of righteousness, and to reprimand the heavenly Watchers.

14 1 The book of the words of righteousness, and of the reprimand of the eternal Watchers in accordance 2 with the command of the Holy Great One in that vision. I saw in my sleep what I will now say with a tongue of flesh and with the breath of my mouth: which the Great One has given to men to 3 converse therewith and understand with the heart As He has created and given to man the power of understanding the word of wisdom, so hath He created me also and given me

the power of reprimanding 4 the Watchers, the children of heaven. I wrote out your petition, and in my vision it appeared thus, that your petition will not be granted unto you throughout all the days of eternity, and that judgment 5 has been has been finally passed upon you: yea (your petition) will not be granted to you and from henceforth you shall not ascend into heaven unto all eternity, and in bonds of the earth the decree 6 has gone forth to bind you for all the days of the world. And (that) previously you shall have seen the destruction of your beloved sons and ye shall have no pleasure in them, but they shall fall before 7 you by the sword. And your petition on their behalf shall not be granted, nor yet on your own: even though you weep and pray and speak all the words contained in the writing which I have 8 written. And the vision was shown to me thus: Behold, in the vision clouds invited me and a mist summoned me, and the course of the stars and the lightnings sped and hastened me, and the winds in 9 the vision caused me to fly and lifted me upward, and bore me into heaven. And I went in till I drew nigh to a wall which is built of crystals and surrounded by tongues of fire: and it began to affright 10 me. And I went into the tongues of fire and drew nigh to a large house which was built of crystals: and the walls of the house were like a tessellated floor (made) of crystals, and its groundwork was 11 of crystal. Its ceiling was like the path of the stars and the lightnings, and between them were 12 fiery cherubim, and their heaven was (clear as) water. A flaming fire surrounded the walls, and its 13 portals blazed with fire. And I entered into that house, and it was hot as fire and cold as ice: there 14 were no delights of life therein: fear covered me, and trembling gat hold upon me. And as I quaked 15 and trembled, I fell upon my face. And I beheld a vision, And lo! there was a second house, greater 16 than the former, and the entire portal stood open before me, and it was built of flames of fire. And in every respect it so excelled in splendour and magnificence and extent that I cannot describe to 17 you its splendour and its extent. And its floor was of fire, and above it were lightnings and the path 18 of the stars, and its ceiling also was flaming fire. And I looked and saw therein a lofty throne: its appearance was as crystal, and the wheels thereof as the shining sun, and there was the vision of 19 cherubim. And from underneath the throne came streams of flaming fire so that I could not look 20 thereon. And the Great Glory sat thereon, and His raiment shone more brightly than the sun and 21 was whiter than any snow. None of the angels could enter and could behold His face by reason 22 of the magnificence and glory, and no flesh could behold Him. The flaming fire was round about Him, and a great fire stood before Him, and none around could draw nigh Him: ten thousand times 23 ten thousand (stood) before Him, yet He needed no counsellor. And the most holy ones who were 24 nigh to Him did not leave by night nor depart from Him. And until then I had been prostrate on my face, trembling: and the Lord called me with His own mouth, and said to me: 'Come hither, Enoch, and hear my word.' And one of the holy ones came to me and waked me, and he made me rise up and approach the door: and I bowed my face downwards.

15:[1] And He answered and said to me, and I heard His voice: ' Fear not, Enoch, thou righteous 2 man and scribe of righteousness: approach hither and hear my voice. And go, say to [the Watchers of heaven] who have sent thee to intercede [for them: "You should intercede for men, and not men 3 for you: Wherefore have ye left the high, holy, and eternal heaven, and lain with women, and defiled yourselves with the daughters of men and taken to yourselves wives, and done like the children 4 of earth, and begotten giants (as your) sons? And though ye were holy, spiritual, living the eternal life, you have defiled yourselves with the blood of women, and have begotten (children) with the blood of flesh, and, as the children of men, have lusted after flesh and blood as those [also] do who die 5 and perish. Therefore have I given them wives also that they might impregnate them, and beget 6 children by them, that thus nothing might be wanting to them on earth. But you were [formerly] 7 spiritual, living the eternal life, and immortal for all generations of the world. And therefore I have not appointed wives for you; for as for the spiritual ones of the heaven, in heaven is their dwelling. 8 And now, the giants, who are produced from the spirits and flesh, shall be called evil spirits upon 9 the earth, and on the earth shall be their dwelling. Evil spirits have proceeded from their bodies; because they are born from men [and] from the holy Watchers is their beginning and primal origin; 10 [they shall be evil spirits on earth, and] evil spirits shall they be called. [As for the spirits of heaven, in heaven shall be their dwelling, but as for the spirits of the earth which were born upon the earth, 11 on the earth shall be their dwelling.] And the spirits of the giants afflict, oppress, destroy, attack, do battle, and work destruction on the earth, and cause trouble: they take no food, [but nevertheless 12 hunger] and thirst, and cause offenses. And these spirits shall rise up against the children of men and against the women, because they have proceeded [from them].

16:1 From the days of the slaughter and destruction and death [of the giants], from the souls of whose flesh the spirits, having gone forth, shall destroy without incurring judgment, thus shall they destroy until the day of the consummation, the great [judgment] in which the age shall be consummated, 2 over the Watchers and the godless, yea, shall be wholly consummated." And now as to the watchers who have sent thee to intercede for them, who had been aforetime in heaven, (say 3 to them): "You have been in heaven, but fall the mysteries had not yet been revealed to you, and you knew worthless ones, and these in the hardness of your hearts you have made known to the women, and through these mysteries women and men work much evil on earth." 4 Say to them therefore: "You have no peace." '

17 1 And they took and brought me to a place in which those who were there were like flaming fire, 2 and, when they wished, they appeared as men. And they brought me to the place of darkness, and 3 to a mountain the point of whose summit reached to heaven. And I saw the places of the luminaries and the treasuries of the stars and of the thunder, and in the uttermost depths, where were 4 a fiery bow and arrows and their quiver, and a fiery sword and all the lightnings. And they took 5 me to the living waters, and to the fire of the west, which receives every setting of the sun. And I came to a river of fire in which the fire flows like water and discharges itself into the great sea towards 6 the west. I saw the great rivers and came to the great river and to the great darkness, and went 7 to the place where no flesh walks. I saw the mountains of the darkness of winter and the place 8 whence all the waters of the deep flow. I saw the mouths of all the rivers of the earth and the mouth of the deep.

18 1 I saw the treasuries of all the winds: I saw how He had furnished with them the whole creation 2 and the firm foundations of the earth. And I saw the corner-stone of the earth: I saw the four 3 winds which bear [the earth and] the firmament of the heaven. And I saw how the winds stretch out the vaults of heaven, and have their station between heaven and earth: these are the pillars 4 of the heaven". I saw the winds of heaven which turn and bring the circumference of the sun and 5 all the stars to their setting. I saw the winds on the earth carrying the clouds: I saw the paths 6 of the angels. I saw at the end of the earth the firmament of the heaven above. And I proceeded and saw a place which burns day and night, where there are seven mountains of magnificent stones, 7 three towards the east, and three towards the south. And as for those towards the east, (one) was of coloured stone, and one of pearl, and one of jacinth, and those towards the south of red stone. 8 But the middle one reached to heaven like the throne of God, of alabaster, and the summit of the 9, 10 throne was of sapphire. And I saw a flaming fire. And beyond these mountains Is a region the 11 end of the great earth: there the heavens were completed. And I saw a deep abyss, with columns of heavenly fire, and among them I saw columns of fire fall, which were beyond measure alike towards 12 the height and towards the depth. And beyond that abyss I saw a place which had no firmament of the heaven above, and no firmly founded earth beneath it: there was no water upon it, and no 13 birds, but it was a waste and horrible place. I saw there seven stars like great burning mountains, 14 and to me, when I inquired regarding them, The angel said: 'This place is the end of heaven and 15 earth: this has become a prison for the stars and the host of heaven. And the stars which roll over the fire are they which have transgressed the commandment of the Lord in the beginning of 16 their rising, because they did not come forth at their appointed times. And He was wroth with them, and bound them till the time when their guilt should be consummated (even) for ten thousand years.'

19 1 And Uriel said to me: 'Here shall stand the angels who have connected themselves with women, and their spirits assuming many different forms are defiling mankind and shall lead them astray into sacrificing to demons as gods", (here shall they stand,) till the day of the great judgement in

2 which they shall be judged till they are made an end of. And the women also of the angels who 3 went astray shall become sirens.' And I, Enoch, alone saw the vision, the ends of all things: and no man shall see as I have seen.

20 1, 2 And these are the names of the holy angels who watch. Uriel, one of the holy angels, who is 3 over the world and over Tartarus. Raphael, one of the holy angels, who is over the spirits of men. 4, 5 Raguel, one of the holy angels who takes vengeance on the world of the luminaries. Michael, one 6 of the holy angels, to wit, he that is set over the best part of mankind and over chaos. Saraqael, 7 one of the holy angels, who is set over the spirits, who sin in the spirit. Gabriel, one of the holy 8 angels, who is over Paradise and the serpents and the Cherubim. Remiel, one of the holy angels, whom God set over those who rise.

21 1, 2 And I proceeded to where things were chaotic. And I saw there something horrible: I saw neither 3 a heaven above nor a firmly founded earth, but a place chaotic and horrible. And there I saw 4 seven stars of the heaven bound together in it, like great mountains and burning with fire. Then 5 I said: 'For what sin are they bound, and on what account have they been cast in hither?' Then said Uriel, one of the holy angels, who was with me, and was chief over them, and said: 'Enoch, why 6 dost thou ask, and why art thou eager for the truth? These are of the number of the stars of heaven, which have transgressed the commandment of the Lord, and are bound here till ten thousand years, 7 the time entailed by their sins, are consummated.' And from thence I went to another place, which was still more horrible than the former, and I saw a horrible thing: a great fire there which burnt and blazed, and the place was cleft as far as the abyss, being full of great descending columns of 8 fire: neither its extent or magnitude could I see, nor could I conjecture.

Then I said: 'How 9 fearful is the place and how terrible to look upon!' Then Uriel answered me, one of the holy angels who was with me: Enoch, why hast thou such fear and affright?' And 10 I answered: 'Because of this fearful place, and because of the spectacle of the pain.' And he said unto me: 'This place is the prison of the angels, and here they will be imprisoned for ever.'

22 1 And thence I went to another place, and he showed me in the west another great and high mountain [and] of hard rock. And there were four hollow places in it, deep 2 and very smooth: three of them were dark and one bright and there was a fountain of water in its midst. And I said how smooth are these hollow places, and deep and dark to view.' 3 Then Raphael answered, one of the holy angels who was with me, and said unto me: 'These hollow places have been created for this very purpose, that the spirits of the souls of the dead should 4 assemble therein, yea that all the souls of the children of men should assemble here. And these places have been made to receive them till the day of their judgment and till their appointed period [till the period appointed], till the great judgement (comes) upon them.' I saw (the spirit of) a dead man making suit, 5 and his voice went forth to heaven and made suit. And I asked Raphael the angel who was 6 with me, and I said unto him: 'This spirit which maketh suit, whose is it, whose voice goeth forth and maketh suit to heaven?' 7 And he answered me saying: 'This is the spirit which went forth from Abel, whom his brother Cain slew, and he makes his suit against him till his seed is destroyed from the face of the earth, and his seed is annihilated from amongst the seed of men.' 8 Then I asked regarding it, and regarding all the hollow places: Why is one separated from the other?' 9 And he answered me and said unto me: 'These three have been made that the spirits of the dead might be separated. And such a division has been made (for) the spirits of the righteous, in which there is the bright spring of water. 10 And such has been made for sinners when they die and are buried in the earth and judgement has not been executed on them in their lifetime. 11 Here their spirits shall be set apart in this great pain till the great day of judgement and punishment and torment of those who curse for ever and retribution for their spirits. There 12 He shall bind them for ever. And such a division has been made for the spirits of those who make their suit, who make disclosures concerning their destruction, when they were slain in the days 13 of the sinners. Such has been made for the spirits of men who were not righteous but sinners, who were complete in transgression, and of the transgressors they shall be companions: but their spirits shall not be slain in the day of judgement nor shall they be raised from thence.' 14 Then I blessed the Lord of glory and said: 'Blessed be my Lord, the Lord of righteousness, who ruleth for ever.'

23 1,2 From thence I went to another place to the west of the ends of the earth. And I saw a burning 3 fire which ran without resting, and paused not from its course day or night but (ran) regularly. And 4 I asked saying: 'What is this which rests not?' Then Raguel, one of the holy angels who was with me, answered me and said unto me: 'This course of fire which thou hast seen is the fire in the west which persecutes all the luminaries of heaven.'

24 1 And from thence I went to another place of the earth, and he showed a mountain range of 2 fire which burnt day and night. And I went beyond it and saw seven magnificent mountains all differing each from the other, and the stones (thereof) were magnificent and beautiful, magnificent as a whole, of glorious appearance and fair exterior: three towards the east, one founded on the other, and three towards the south, one upon the other, and deep rough ravines, no one of which 3 joined with any other. And the seventh mountain was in the midst of these and it excelled them 4 in height, resembling the seat of a throne: and fragrant trees encircled the throne. And amongst them was a tree such as I had never yet smelt, neither was any amongst them nor were others like it: it had a fragrance beyond all fragrance, and its leaves and blooms and wood wither not for ever: 5 and its fruit is beautiful, and its fruit resembles the dates of a palm. Then I said: 'How beautiful is this tree, and fragrant, and its leaves are fair, and its blooms very delightful in appearance.' 6 Then answered Michael, one of the holy and honoured angels who was with me, and was their leader.

25 1 And he said unto me: 'Enoch,why dost thou ask me regarding the fragrance of the tree, 2 and why dost thou wish to learn the truth?' Then I answered him saying: 'I wish to 3 know about everything, but especially about this tree.' And he answered saying: 'This high mountain which thou hast seen, whose summit is like the throne of God, His throne, where the Holy Great One, the Lord of Glory, the Eternal King, will sit, when He shall come down to visit 4 the earth with goodness. And as for this fragrant tree no mortal is permitted to touch it till the great judgement, when He shall take vengeance on all and bring (everything) its consummation 5 for ever. It shall then be given to the righteous and holy. Its fruit shall be for food to the elect: it shall be transplanted to the holy place, to the temple of the Lord, the Eternal King. 6 Then shall they rejoice with joy and be glad, And into the holy place shall they enter; And its fragrance shall be in their bones, And they shall live a long life on earth, Such as thy fathers lived: And in their days shall no sorrow or plague Or torment or calamity touch them.' Then blessed I the God of Glory, the Eternal King, who hath prepared such things for the righteous, and hath created them and promised to give to them.

26 1 And I went from thence to the middle of the earth, and I saw a blessed place in which there were 2 trees with branches abiding and blooming [of a dismembered tree]. And there I saw a holy mountain, 3 and underneath the mountain to the east there was a stream and it flowed towards the south. And I saw towards the east another mountain higher than this, and between them a deep and narrow 4 ravine: in it also ran a stream underneath the mountain. And to the west thereof there was another mountain, lower than the former and of small elevation, and a ravine deep and dry between 5 them: and another deep and dry ravine was at the extremities of the three mountains. And all the ravines were deep and narrow, (being formed) of hard rock, and trees were not planted upon 6 them. And I marvelled at the rocks, and I marvelled at the ravine, yea, I marvelled very much.

27 1 Then said I: 'For what object is this blessed land, which is entirely filled with trees, and this 2 accursed valley between? 'Then Uriel, one of the holy angels who was with me, answered and said: "This accursed valley is for those who are accursed for ever: here shall all the accursed be gathered together who utter with their lips against the Lord unseemly words and of His glory speak hard things. Here shall they be gathered together, and here 3 shall be their place of judgement. In the last days there shall be upon them the spectacle of righteous judgement in the presence of the righteous for ever: here shall the merciful bless the Lord of glory, the Eternal King. 4 In the days of judgement over the former, they shall bless Him for the mercy in accordance with 5 which He has assigned them (their lot).' Then I blessed the Lord of Glory and set forth His glory and lauded Him gloriously.

28 1 And thence I went towards the east, into the midst of the mountain range of the desert, and 2 I saw a wilderness and it was solitary, full of trees and plants. And water gushed forth from 3 above. Rushing like a copious watercourse [which flowed] towards the north-west it caused clouds and dew to ascend on every side.

29 1 And thence I went to another place in the desert, and approached to the east of this mountain 2 range. And there I saw aromatic trees exhaling the fragrance of frankincense and myrrh, and the trees also were similar to the almond tree.

30 1, 2 And beyond these, I went afar to the east, and I saw another place, a valley (full) of water. And 3 therein there was a tree, the colour (?) of fragrant trees such as the mastic. And on the sides of those valleys I saw fragrant cinnamon. And beyond these I proceeded to the east.

31 1 And I saw other mountains, and amongst them were groves of trees, and there flowed forth from 2 them nectar which is named sarara and galbanum And beyond these mountains I saw another mountain to the east of the ends of the earth, whereon were aloe trees, and all the trees were full 3 of stacte, being like almond-trees. And when one burnt it, it smelt sweeter than any fragrant odour.

32 1 And after these fragrant odours, as I looked seven mountains full of choice nard and fragrant trees and cinnamon and pepper. 2 And thence I went over the summits of all these mountains, far towards the east of the earth, and passed above the Erythraean sea and went far from it, and passed over the angel Zotiel. 3 And I came to the Garden of

Righteousness; and saw beyond those trees many large trees growing there and of goodly fragrance, large, very beautiful and glorious, and the tree of I wisdom whereof they eat and know great wisdom. 4. That tree is in height like the fir, and its leaves are like (those of) the Carob tree: and its fruit 5 is like the clusters of the vine, very beautiful: and the fragrance of the tree penetrates afar. Then 6 I said: How beautiful is the tree, and how attractive is its look!' Then Raphael the holy angel, who was with me, answered me and said: 'This is the tree of wisdom, of which thy father old (in years) and thy aged mother, who were before thee, have eaten, and they learnt wisdom and their eyes were opened, and they knew that they were naked and they were driven out of the garden.'

33 1 And from thence I went to the ends of the earth and saw there great beasts, and each differed from the other; and (I saw) birds also differing in appearance and beauty and voice, the one differing from the other. And to the east of those beasts I saw the ends of the earth whereon the heaven 2 rests, and the portals of the heaven open. And I saw how the stars of heaven come forth, and 3 I counted the portals out of which they proceed, and wrote down all their outlets, of each individual star by itself, according to their number and their names, their courses and their positions, and their 4 times and their months, as Uriel the holy angel who was with me showed me. He showed all things to me and wrote them down for me: also their names he wrote for me, and their laws and their companies.

34 1 And from thence I went towards the north to the ends of the earth, and there I saw a great and 2 glorious device at the ends of the whole earth. And here I saw three portals of heaven open in the heaven: through each of them proceed north winds: when they blow there is cold, hail, frost, 3 snow, dew, and rain. And out of one portal they blow for good: but when they blow through the other two portals, it is with violence and affliction on the earth, and they blow with violence.

35 And from thence I went towards the west to the ends of the earth, and saw there three portals of the heaven open such as I had seen in the east, the same number of portals, and the same number of outlets.

36 1 And from thence I went to the south to the ends of the earth, and saw there three open portals 2 of the heaven: and thence there come dew, rain, and wind. And from thence I went to the east to the ends of the heaven, and saw here the three eastern portals of heaven open and small portals 3 above them. Through each of these small portals pass the stars of heaven and run their course 4 to the west on the path which is shown to them. And as often as I saw I blessed always the Lord of Glory, and I continued to bless the Lord of Glory who has wrought great and glorious wonders, to show the greatness of His work to the angels and to spirits and to men, that they might praise His work and all His creation: that they might see the work of His might and praise the great work of His hands and bless Him for ever.

The Parables

37 1 The second vision which he saw, the vision of wisdom -which Enoch the son of Jared, the son 2 of Mahalalel, the son of Cainan, the son of Enos, the son of Seth, the son of Adam, saw. And this is the beginning of the words of wisdom which I lifted up my voice to speak and say to those which dwell on earth: Hear, ye men of old time, and see, ye that come after, the words of the Holy 3 One which I will speak before the Lord of Spirits. It were better to declare (them only) to the men of old time, but even from those that come after we will not withhold the beginning of wisdom. 4 Till the present day such wisdom has never been given by the Lord of Spirits as I have received according to my insight, according to the good pleasure of the Lord of Spirits by whom the lot of 5 eternal life has been given to me. Now three Parables were imparted to me, and I lifted up my voice and recounted them to those that dwell on the earth.

38 1 The first Parable. When the congregation of the righteous shall appear, And sinners shall be judged for their sins, And shall be driven from the face of the earth: 2 And when the Righteous One shall appear before the eyes of the righteous, Whose elect works hang upon the Lord of Spirits, And light shall appear to the righteous and the elect who dwell on the earth, Where then will be the dwelling of the sinners, And where the resting-place of those who have denied the Lord of Spirits? It had been good for them if they had not been born. 3 When the secrets of the righteous shall be revealed and the sinners judged, And the godless driven from the presence of the righteous and elect, 4 From that time those that possess the earth shall no longer be powerful and exalted: And they shall not be able to behold the face of the holy, For the Lord of Spirits has caused His light to appear On the face of the holy, righteous, and elect. 5 Then shall the kings and the mighty perish And be given into the hands of the righteous and holy. 6 And thenceforward none shall seek for themselves mercy from the Lord of Spirits For their life is at an end.

39 1 [And it shall come to pass in those days that elect and holy children will descend from the 2 high heaven, and their seed will become one with the children of men. And in those days Enoch received books of zeal and wrath, and books of disquiet and expulsion.] And mercy shall not be accorded to them, saith the Lord of Spirits. 3 And in those days a whirlwind carried me off from the earth, And set me down at the end of the heavens. 4 And there I saw another vision, the dwelling-places of the holy, And the resting-places of the righteous. 5 Here mine eyes saw their dwellings with His righteous angels, And their resting-places with the holy. And they petitioned and interceded and prayed for the children of men, And righteousness flowed before them as water, And mercy like dew upon the earth: Thus it is amongst them for ever and ever. 6a And in that place mine eyes saw the Elect One of righteousness and of faith, 7b And all the righteous and elect before Him shall be strong as fiery lights, And their mouth shall be full of blessing, And their lips extol the name of the Lord of Spirits, And righteousness before Him shall never fail And uprightness shall never fail before Him.] 8 There I wished to dwell, And my spirit longed for that dwelling-place: And there heretofore hath been my portion, For so has it been established concerning me before the Lord of Spirits. 9 In those days I praised and extolled the name of the Lord of Spirits with blessings and praises, because He hath destined me for blessing and glory according to the good pleasure of the Lord of of Spirits. For a long time my eyes regarded that place, and blessed Him and praised Him, saying: 11 'Blessed is He, and may He be blessed from the beginning and for evermore. And before Him there is no ceasing. He knows before the world was created what is for ever and what will be from 12 generation unto generation. Those who sleep not bless Thee: they stand before Thy glory and bless, praise, and extol, saying: "Holy, holy; holy, is the Lord of Spirits: He filleth the earth with 13 spirits." 'And here my eyes saw all those who sleep not: they stand before Him and bless and say: 14 'Blessed be Thou, and blessed be the name of the Lord for ever and ever.' And my face was changed; for I could nolonger behold.

40 1 And after that I saw thousands of thousands and ten thousand times ten thousand, I saw a multitude 2 beyond number and reckoning, who stood before the Lord of Spirits. And on the four sides of the Lord of Spirits I saw four presences, different from those that sleep not, and I learnt their names: for the angel that went with me made known to me their names, and showed me all the hidden things. 3 And I heard the voices of those four presences as they uttered praises before the Lord of glory. 4, 5 The first voice blesses the Lord of Spirits for ever and ever, And the second voice I heard blessing 6 the Elect One and the elect ones who hang upon the Lord of Spirits. And the third voice I heard pray and intercede for those who dwell on the earth and supplicate in the name of the Lord of Spirits. 7 And I heard the fourth voice fending off the Satans and forbidding them to come before the Lord 8 of Spirits to accuse them who dwell on the earth. After that I asked the angel of peace who went with me, who showed me everything that is hidden: 'Who are these four presences which I have 9 seen and whose words I have heard and written down? 'And he said to me: 'This first is Michael, the merciful and long-suffering: and the second, who is set over all the diseases and all the wounds of the children of men, is Raphael: and the third who is set over all the powers, is Gabriel: and the fourth, who is set over the repentance unto hope of those who inherit eternal life, is named Phanuel.' 10 And these are the four angels of the Lord of Spirits and the four voices I heard in those days.

41 1 And after that I saw all the secrets of the heavens, and how the kingdom is divided, and how the 2 actions of men are weighed in the balance. And there I saw the mansions of the elect and the mansions of the holy, and mine eyes saw there all the sinners being driven from thence which deny the name of the Lord of Spirits, and being dragged off: and they could not abide because of the punishment which proceeds from the Lord of Spirits. 3 And there mine eyes saw the secrets of thunder, and the secrets of the winds, how they are divided to blow over the earth and the secrets of the clouds and dew, and there 4 I saw from whence they proceed in that place from whence they saturate the dusty earth. And there I saw closed chambers out of which the winds are divided, the chamber of the hail and winds, the chamber of the mist, and of the clouds, and the cloud thereof hovers over the earth from the 5 beginning of the world.' And I saw the chambers of the sun and moon, whence they proceed and whither they come again, and their glorious return, and how one is superior to the other, and their stately orbit, and how they do not leave their orbit, and they add nothing to their orbit and they take nothing from it, and they keep faith with each other, in accordance with the oath by which they 6 are bound together. And first the sun goes forth and traverses his path according to the commandment 7 of the Lord of Spirits, and mighty is His name for ever and ever. And after that I saw the hidden and the visible path of the moon, and she accomplishes the course of her path in that place by day and by night the one holding a position opposite to the other before the Lord of Spirits. And they give thanks and praise and rest not For unto them is their thanksgiving rest, 8 For the sun changes oft for a blessing or a curse, And the course of the .path of the moon is light to the righteous And darkness to the sinners in the name of the Lord Who made a separation between the light and the darkness And divided the spirits of men, And strengthened the spirits of the righteous In the name of His righteousness. 9 For no angel hinders and no power is able to hinder; for He appoints a judge for them all and He judges them all before Him.

42 1 Wisdom found no place where she might dwell; Then a dwelling-place was assigned her in the heavens. 2 Wisdom went forth to make her dwelling among the children of men, And found no dwelling-place: Wisdom returned to her place, And took her seat among the angels. 3 And unrighteousness went forth from her chambers: Whom she sought not she found, And dwelt with them, As rain in a desert And dew on a thirsty land.

43 1 And I saw other lightnings and the stars of heaven, and I saw how He called them all by their 2 names and they hearkened unto Him. And I saw how they are weighed in a righteous balance according to their proportions of light: (I saw) the width of their spaces and the day of their appearing, and how their revolution produces lightning: and (I saw) their revolution according to the 3 number of the angels, and (how) they keep faith with each other. And I asked the angel who went 4 with me who showed me what was hidden: 'What are these?' And he said to me: 'The Lord of Spirits hath showed thee their parabolic meaning (lit. 'their parable'): these are the names of the holy who dwell on the earth and believe in the name of the Lord of Spirits for ever and ever.'

44 Also another phenomenon I saw in regard to the lightnings: how some of the stars arise and become lightnings and cannot part with their new form.

45 1 And this is the second Parable concerning those who deny the name of the dwelling of the holy ones and the Lord of Spirits. 2 And into the heaven they shall not ascend, And on the earth they shall not come: Such shall be the lot of the sinners Who have denied the name of the Lord of Spirits, Who are thus preserved for the day of suffering and tribulation. 3 On that day Mine Elect One shall sit on the throne of glory And shall try their works, And their places of rest shall be innumerable. And their souls shall grow strong within them when they see Mine elect ones, And those who have called upon My glorious name: 4 Then will I cause Mine Elect One to dwell among them. And I will transform the heaven and make it an eternal blessing and light: And I will transform the earth and make it a blessing: 5 And I will cause Mine elect ones to dwell upon it: But the sinners and evil-doers shall not set foot thereon. 6 For I have provided and satisfied with peace My righteous ones And have caused them to dwell before Me: But for the sinners there is judgement impending with Me, So that I shall destroy them from the face of the earth.

46 1 And there I saw One who had a head of days, And His head was white like wool, And with Him was another being whose countenance had the appearance of a man, And his face was full of graciousness, like one of the holy angels 2 And I asked the angel who went with me and showed me all the hidden things, concerning that 3 Son of man, who he was, and whence he was, (and) why he went with the Head of days? And he answered and said unto me: This is the Son of Man who hath righteousness, With whom dwelleth righteousness, And who revealeth all the treasures of that which is hidden, Because the Lord of Spirits hath chosen him, And whose lot hath the pre-eminence before the Lord of Spirits in uprightness for ever. 4 And this Son of Man whom thou hast seen Shall raise up the kings and the mighty from their seats, [And the strong from their thrones] And shall loosen the reins of the strong, And break the teeth of the sinners. [And he shall put down the kings from their thrones and kingdoms] Because they do not extol and praise Him, Nor humbly acknowledge whence the kingdom was bestowed upon them. 6 And he shall put down the countenance of the strong, And shall fill them with shame.

And darkness shall be their dwelling, And worms shall be their bed, And they shall have no hope of rising from their beds, Because they do not extol the name of the Lord of Spirits. 7 And these are they who judge the stars of heaven, [And raise their hands against the Most High], And tread upon the earth and dwell upon it. And all their deeds manifest unrighteousness, And their power rests upon their riches, And their faith is in the gods which they have made with their hands, And they deny the name of the Lord of Spirits, 8 And they persecute the houses of His congregations, And the faithful who hang upon the name of the Lord of Spirits.

47 1 And in those days shall have ascended the prayer of the righteous, And the blood of the righteous from the earth before the Lord of Spirits. In those days the holy ones who dwell above in the heavens Shall unite with one voice And supplicate and pray [and praise, And give thanks and bless the name of the Lord of Spirits] On behalf of the blood of the righteous which has been shed, And that the prayer of the righteous may not be in vain before the Lord of Spirits, That judgement may be done unto them, And that they may not have to suffer for ever. In those days I saw the Head of Days when He seated himself upon the throne of His glory, And the books of the living were opened before Him: And all His host which is in heaven above and His counsellors stood before Him, And the hearts of the holy were filled with joy; Because the number of the righteous had been offered, And the prayer of the righteous had been heard, And the blood of the righteous been required before the Lord of Spirits.

48 1 And in that place I saw the fountain of righteousness Which was inexhaustible: And around it were many fountains of wisdom: And all the thirsty drank of them, And were filled with wisdom, And their dwellings were with the righteous and holy and elect. 2 And at that hour that Son of Man was named In the presence of the Lord of Spirits, And his name before the Head of Days. 3 Yea, before the sun and the signs were created, Before the stars of the heaven were made, His name was named before the Lord of Spirits. 4 He shall be a staff to the righteous whereon to stay themselves and not fall, And he shall be the light of the Gentiles, And the hope of those who are troubled of heart. 5 All who dwell on earth shall fall down and worship before him, And will praise and bless and celebrate with song the Lord of Spirits. 6 And for this reason hath he been chosen and hidden before Him; Before the creation of the world and for evermore. 7 And the wisdom of the Lord of Spirits hath revealed him to the holy and righteous; For he hath preserved the lot of the righteous, Because they have hated and despised this world of unrighteousness, And have hated all its works and ways in the name of the Lord of Spirits: For in his name they are saved, And according to his good pleasure hath it been in regard to their life. 8 In these days downcast in countenance shall the kings of the earth have become, And the strong who possess the land because of the works of their hands, For on the day of their anguish and affliction they shall not (be able to) save themselves. 9 And I will give them over into the hands of Mine elect: As straw in the fire so shall they burn before the face of the holy: As lead in the water shall they sink before the face of the righteous, And no trace of them shall any more be found. 10 And on the day of their affliction there shall be rest on the earth, And before them they shall fall and not rise again: And there shall be no one to take them with his hands and raise them:For they have denied the Lord of Spirits and His Anointed. The name of the Lord of Spirits be blessed.

49 1 For wisdom is poured out like water, And glory faileth not before him for evermore. 2 For he is mighty in all the secrets of righteousness, And unrighteousness shall disappear as a shadow, And have no continuance; Because the Elect One standeth before the Lord of Spirits, And his glory is for ever and ever, And his might unto all generations. 3 And in him dwells the spirit of wisdom, And the spirit which gives insight, And the spirit of understanding and of might, And the spirit of those who have fallen asleep in righteousness. 4 And he shall judge the secret things, And none shall be able to utter a lying word before him; For he is the Elect One before the Lord of Spirits according to His good pleasure.

50 1 And in those days a change shall take place for the holy and elect, And the light of days shall abide upon them, And glory and honour shall turn to the holy, 2 On the day of affliction on which evil shall have been treasured up against the sinners. And the righteous shall be victorious in the name of the Lord of Spirits: And He will cause the others to witness (this) That they may repent And forgo the works of their hands. 3 They shall have no honour through the name of the Lord of Spirits, Yet through His name shall they be saved, And the Lord of Spirits will have compassion on them, For His compassion is great. 4 And He is righteous also in His judgement, And in the presence of His glory unrighteousness also shall not maintain itself: At His judgement the unrepentant shall perish before Him. 5 And from henceforth I will have no mercy on them, saith the Lord of Spirits.

51 1 And in those days shall the earth also give back that which has been entrusted to it, And Sheol also shall give back that which it has received, And hell shall give back that which it owes. 5a For in those days the Elect One shall arise,

2 And he shall choose the righteous and holy from among them: For the day has drawn nigh that they should be saved. 3 And the Elect One shall in those days sit on My throne, And his mouth shall pour forth all the secrets of wisdom and counsel: For the Lord of Spirits hath given (them) to him and hath glorified him. 4 And in those days shall the mountains leap like rams, And the hills also shall skip like lambs satisfied with milk, And the faces of [all] the angels in heaven shall be lighted up with joy. 5b And the earth shall rejoice, c And the righteous shall dwell upon it, d And the elect shall walk thereon.

52 1 And after those days in that place where I had seen all the visions of that which is hidden for 2 I had been carried off in a whirlwind and they had borne me towards the west There mine eyes saw all the secret things of heaven that shall be, a mountain of iron, and a mountain of copper, and a mountain of silver, and a mountain of gold, and a mountain of soft metal, and a mountain of lead. 3 And I asked the angel who went with me, saying, 'What things are these which I have seen in 4 secret?' And he said unto me: 'All these things which thou hast seen shall serve the dominion of His Anointed that he may be potent and mighty on the earth.' 5 And that angel of peace answered, saying unto me: 'Wait a little, and there shall be revealed unto thee all the secret things which surround the Lord of Spirits. 6 And these mountains which thine eyes have seen, The mountain of iron, and the mountain of copper, and the mountain of silver, And the mountain of gold, and the mountain of soft metal, and the mountain of lead, All these shall be in the presence of the Elect One As wax before the fire, And like the water which streams down from above [upon those mountains], And they shall become powerless before his feet. 7 And it shall come to pass in those days that none shall be saved, Either by gold or by silver, And none be able to escape. 8

And there shall be no iron for war, Nor shall one clothe oneself with a breastplate. Bronze shall be of no service, And tin [shall be of no service and] shall not be esteemed, And lead shall not be desired. 9 And all these things shall be [denied and] destroyed from the surface of the earth, When the Elect One shall appear before the face of the Lord of Spirits.'

53 1 There mine eyes saw a deep valley with open mouths, and all who dwell on the earth and sea and islands shall bring to him gifts and presents and tokens of homage, but that deep valley shall not become full. 2 And their hands commit lawless deeds, And the sinners devour all whom they lawlessly oppress: Yet the sinners shall be destroyed before the face of the Lord of Spirits, And they shall be banished from off the face of His earth, And they shall perish for ever and ever. 3 For I saw all the angels of punishment abiding (there) and preparing all the instruments of Satan. 4 And I asked the angel of peace who went with me: 'For whom are they preparing these instruments?' 5 And he said unto me: 'They prepare these for the kings and the mighty of this earth, that they may thereby be destroyed. 6 And after this the Righteous and Elect One shall cause the house of his congregation to appear: henceforth they shall be no more hindered in the name of the Lord of Spirits. 7 And these mountains shall not stand as the earth before his righteousness, But the hills shall be as a fountain of water, And the righteous shall have rest from the oppression of sinners.'

54 1 And I looked and turned to another part of the earth, and saw there a deep valley with burning 2 fire. And they brought the kings and the mighty, and began to cast them into this deep valley. 3 And there mine eyes saw how they made these their instruments, iron chains of immeasurable weight. 4 And I asked the angel of peace who went with me, saying: 'For whom are these chains being prepared?' 5 And .he said unto me: ' These are being prepared for the hosts of Azazel, so that they may take them and cast them into the abyss of complete condemnation, and they shall cover their jaws with rough stones as the Lord of Spirits commanded. 6 And Michael, and Gabriel, and Raphael, and Phanuel shall take hold of them on that great day, and cast them on that day into the burning furnace, that the Lord of Spirits may take vengeance on them for their unrighteousness in becoming subject to Satan and leading astray those who dwell on the earth.' 7 And in those days shall punishment come from the Lord of Spirits, and He will open all the chambers of waters which are above the heavens, and of the fountains which are beneath the earth. 8 And all the waters shall be joined with the waters: that which is above the heavens is the masculine, 9 and the water which is beneath the earth is the feminine. And they shall destroy all who dwell 10 on the earth and those who dwell under the ends of the heaven. And when they have recognized their unrighteousness which they have wrought on the earth, then by these shall they perish.'

55 1 And after that the Head of Days repented and said: 'In vain have I destroyed all who dwell 2 on the earth.' And He sware by His great name: 'Henceforth I will not do so to all who dwell on the earth, and I will set a sign in the heaven: and this shall be a pledge of good faith between Me and them for ever, so long as heaven is above the earth. And this is in accordance with My command. 3 When I have desired to take hold of them by the hand of the angels on the day of tribulation and pain because of this, I will cause My chastisement and My wrath to abide upon them, saith 4 God, the Lord of Spirits. Yet mighty kings who dwell on the earth, ye shall have to behold Mine Elect One, how he sits on the throne of glory and judges Azazel, and all his associates, and all his hosts in the name of the Lord of Spirits.'

56 1 And I saw there the hosts of the angels of punishment going, and they held scourges and chains 2 of iron and bronze. And I asked the angel of peace who went with me, saying: 'To whom are 3 these who hold the scourges going? 'And he said unto me: 'To their elect and beloved ones, that they may be cast into the chasm of the abyss of the valley. 4 And then that valley shall be filled with their elect and beloved, And the days of their lives shall be at an end, And the days of their leading astray shall not thenceforward be reckoned. 5 And in those days the angels shall return And hurl themselves to the east upon the Parthians and Medes: They shall stir up the kings, so that a spirit of unrest shall come upon them, And they shall rouse them from their thrones, That they may break forth as lions from their lairs, And as hungry wolves among their flocks. 6 And they shall go up and tread under foot the land of His elect ones, [And the land of His elect ones shall be before them a threshing-floor and a highway:] 7 But the city of my righteous shall be a hindrance to their horses. And they shall begin to fight among themselves, And their right hand shall be strong against themselves, And a man shall not know his brother, Nor a son his father or his mother, Till there be no number of the corpses through their slaughter, And their punishment be not in vain. 8 In those days Sheol shall open its jaws, And they shall be swallowed up therein, And their destruction shall be at an end; Sheol shall devour the sinners in the presence of the elect.'

57 1 And it came to pass after this that I saw another host of wagons, and men riding thereon, and 2 coming on the winds from the east, and from the west to the south. And the noise of their wagons was heard, and when this turmoil took place the holy ones from heaven remarked it, and the pillars of the earth were moved from their place, and the sound thereof was heard from the one end of heaven 3 to the other in one day. And they shall all fall down and worship before the Lord of Spirits. And this is the end of the second parable.

58 1 And I began to speak the third Parable concerning the righteous and elect. 2 Blessed are ye, ye righteous and elect, For glorious shall be your lot. 3 And the righteous shall be in the light of the sun, And the elect in the light of eternal life: The days of their life shall be unending, And the days of the holy without number. 4 And they shall seek the light and find righteousness with the Lord of Spirits: There shall be peace to the righteous in the name of the Eternal Lord. 5 And after this it shall be said to the holy in heaven That they should seek out the secrets of righteousness, the heritage of faith: For it has become bright as the sun upon earth, And the darkness is past. 6 And there shall be a light that never endeth, And to a limit (lit. 'number') of days they shall not come, For the darkness shall first have been destroyed, [And the light established before the Lord of Spirits] And the light of uprightness established for ever before the Lord of Spirits.

59 1 [In those days mine eyes saw the secrets of the lightnings, and of the lights, and the judgements they execute (lit. 'their judgement'): and they lighten for a blessing or a curse as the Lord of 2 Spirits willeth. And there I saw the secrets of the thunder, and how when it resounds above in the heaven, the sound thereof is heard, and he caused me to see the judgements executed on the earth, whether they be for well-being and blessing, or for a curse according to the word of the Lord of Spirits. 3 And after that all the secrets of the lights and lightnings were shown to me, and they lighten for blessing and for satisfying.]

60 1 In the year 500, in the seventh month, on the fourteenth day of the month in the life of Enoch. In that Parable I saw how a mighty quaking made the heaven of heavens to quake, and the host of the Most High, and the angels, a thousand thousands and ten thousand times ten thousand, were 2 disquieted with a great disquiet. And the Head of Days sat on the throne of His glory, and the angels and the righteous stood around Him. 3 And a great trembling seized me, And fear took hold of me, And my loins gave way, And dissolved were my reins, And I fell upon my face. 4 And Michael sent another angel from among the holy ones and he raised me up, and when he had raised me up my spirit returned; for I had not been able to endure the look of this host, and the 5 commotion and the quaking of the heaven. And Michael said unto me: 'Why art thou disquieted with such a vision? Until this day lasted the day of His mercy; and He hath been merciful and 6 long-suffering towards those who dwell on the earth. And when the day, and the power, and the punishment, and the judgement come, which the Lord of Spirits hath prepared for those who worship not the righteous law, and for those who deny the righteous judgement, and for those who take His name in vain that day is prepared, for the elect a covenant, but for sinners an inquisition. 25 When the punishment of the Lord of Spirits shall rest upon them, it shall rest in order that the punishment of the Lord of Spirits may not come, in vain, and it shall slay the children with their mothers and the children with their fathers. Afterwards the judgement shall take place according to His mercy and His patience.' 7 And on that day were two monsters parted, a female monster named Leviathan, to dwell in the 8 abysses of the ocean over the fountains of the waters. But the male is named

Behemoth, who occupied with his breast a waste wilderness named Duidain on the east of the garden where the elect and righteous dwell, where my grandfather was taken up, the seventh from Adam, the first 9 man whom the Lord of Spirits created. And I besought the other angel that he should show me the might of those monsters, how they were parted on one day and cast, the one into the abysses 10 of the sea, and the other unto the dry land of the wilderness. And he said to me: ' Thou son of man, herein thou dost seek to know what is hidden.' 11 And the other angel who went with me and showed me what was hidden told me what is first and last in the heaven in the height, and beneath the earth in the depth, and at the ends of the 12 heaven, and on the foundation of the heaven. And the chambers of the winds, and how the winds are divided, and how they are weighed, and (how) the portals of the winds are reckoned, each according to the power of the wind, and the power of the lights of the moon, and according to the power that is fitting: and the divisions of the stars according to their names, and how all the divisions 13 are divided. And the thunders according to the places where they fall, and all the divisions that are made among the lightnings that it may lighten, and their host that they may at once obey. 14 For the thunder has places of rest (which) are assigned (to it) while it is waiting for its peal; and the thunder and lightning are inseparable, and although not one and undivided, they both go together 15 through the spirit and separate not. For when the lightning lightens, the thunder utters its voice, and the spirit enforces a pause during the peal, and divides equally between them; for the treasury of their peals is like the sand, and each one of them as it peals is held in with a bridle, and turned back by the power of the spirit, and pushed forward according to the many quarters of the earth. 16 And the spirit of the sea is masculine and strong, and according to the might of his strength he draws it back with a rein, and in like manner it is driven forward and disperses amid all the mountains 17 of the earth. And the spirit of the hoar-frost is his own angel, and the spirit of the hail is a good 18 angel. And the spirit of the snow has forsaken his chambers on account of his strength-- There is a 19 special spirit therein, and that which ascends from it is like smoke, and its name is frost. And the spirit of the mist is not united with them in their chambers, but it has a special chamber; for its course is glorious both in light and in darkness, and in winter and in summer, and in its chamber is an angel. 20 And the spirit of the dew has its dwelling at the ends of the heaven, and is connected with the chambers of the rain, and its course is in winter and summer: and its clouds and the clouds of the 21 mist are connected, and the one gives to the other. And when the spirit of the rain goes forth from its chamber, the angels come and open the chamber and lead it out, and when it is diffused over the whole earth it unites with the water on the earth. And whensoever it unites with the water on 22 the earth... For the waters are for those who dwell on the earth; for they are nourishment for the earth from the Most High who is in heaven: therefore there is a measure for the rain, 23 and the angels take it in charge. And these things I saw towards the Garden of the Righteous. 24 And the angel of peace who was with me said to me: 'These two monsters, prepared conformably to the greatness of God, shall feed...

61 1 And I saw in those days how long cords were given to those angels, and they took to themselves wings and flew, and they went towards the north. 2 And I asked the angel, saying unto him: 'Why have those (angels) taken these cords and gone off?' And he said unto me: 'They have gone to measure.' 3 And the angel who went with me said unto me: 'These shall bring the measures of the righteous, And the ropes of the righteous to the righteous, That they may stay themselves on the name of the Lord of Spirits for ever and ever. 4 The elect shall begin to dwell with the elect, And those are the measures which shall be given to faith And which shall strengthen righteousness. 5 And these measures shall reveal all the secrets of the depths of the earth, And those who have been destroyed by the desert, And those who have been devoured by the beasts, And those who have been devoured by the fish of the sea, That they may return and stay themselves On the day of the Elect One; For none shall be destroyed before the Lord of Spirits, And none can be destroyed. 6 And all who dwell above in the heaven received a command and power and one voice and one light like unto fire. 7 And that One (with) their first words they blessed, And extolled and lauded with wisdom, And they were wise in utterance and in the spirit of life. 8 And the Lord of Spirits placed the Elect One on the throne of glory. And he shall judge all the works of the holy above in the heaven, And in the balance shall their deeds be weighed. 9 And when he shall lift up his countenance To judge their secret ways according to the word of the name of the Lord of Spirits, And their path according to the way of the righteous judgement of the Lord of Spirits, Then shall they all with one voice speak and bless, And glorify and extol and sanctify the name of the Lord of Spirits. 10 And He will summon all the host of the heavens, and all the holy ones above, and the host of God, the Cherubin, Seraphin and Ophannin, and all the angels of power, and all the angels of principalities, 11 and the Elect One, and the other powers on the earth (and) over the water On that day shall raise one voice, and bless and glorify and exalt in the spirit of faith, and in the spirit of wisdom, and in the spirit of patience, and in the spirit of mercy, and in the spirit of judgement and of peace, and in the spirit of goodness, and shall all say with one voice: "Blessed is He, and may the name of the Lord of

Spirits be blessed for ever and ever." 12 All who sleep not above in heaven shall bless Him: All the holy ones who are in heaven shall bless Him. And all the elects who dwell in the garden of life: And every spirit of light who is able to bless, and glorify, and extol, and hallow Thy blessed name, And all flesh shall beyond measure glorify and bless Thy name for ever and ever. 13 For great is the mercy of the Lord of Spirits, and He is long-suffering, And all His works and all that He has created He has revealed to the righteous and elect In the name of the Lord of Spirits.'

62 1 And thus the Lord commanded the kings and the mighty and the exalted, and those who dwell on the earth, and said: 'Open your eyes and lift up your horns if ye are able to recognize the Elect One.' 2 And the Lord of Spirits seated him on the throne of His glory, And the spirit of righteousness was poured out upon him, And the word of his mouth slays all the sinners, And all the unrighteous are destroyed from before his face. 3 And there shall stand up in that day all the kings and the mighty, And the exalted and those who hold the earth, And they shall see and recognize How he sits on the throne of his glory, And righteousness is judged before him, And no lying word is spoken before him. 4 Then shall pain come upon them as on a woman in travail, [And she has pain in bringing forth] When her child enters the mouth of the womb, And she has pain in bringing forth. 5 And one portion of them shall look on the other, And they shall be terrified, And they shall be downcast of countenance, And pain shall seize them, When they see that Son of Man Sitting on the throne of his glory. 6 And the kings and the mighty and all who possess the earth shall bless and glorify and extol him who rules over all, who was hidden. 7 For from the beginning the Son of Man was hidden, And the Most High preserved him in the presence of His might, And revealed him to the elect. 8 And the congregation of the elect and holy shall be sown. And all the elect shall stand before him on that day. 9 And all the kings and the mighty and the exalted and those who rule the earth Shall fall down before him on their faces, And worship and set their hope upon that Son of Man, And petition him and supplicate for mercy at his hands. 10 Nevertheless that Lord of Spirits will so press them That they shall hastily go forth from His presence, And their faces shall be filled with shame, And the darkness grow deeper on their faces. 11 And He will deliver them to the angels for punishment, To execute vengeance on them because they have oppressed His children and His elect 12 And they shall be a spectacle for the righteous and for His elect: They shall rejoice over them, Because the wrath of the Lord of Spirits resteth upon them, And His sword is drunk with their blood. 13 And the righteous and elect shall be saved on that day, And they shall never thence forward see the face of the sinners and unrighteous. 14 And the Lord of Spirits will abide over them, And with that Son of Man shall they eat And lie down and rise up for ever and ever. 15 And the righteous and elect shall have risen from the earth, And ceased to be of downcast countenance. And they shall have been clothed with garments of glory, 16 And these shall be the garments of life from the Lord of Spirits: And your garments shall not grow old, Nor your glory pass away before the Lord of Spirits.

63 1 In those days shall the mighty and the kings who possess the earth implore (Him) to grant them a little respite from His angels of punishment to whom they were delivered, that they might fall 2 down and worship before the Lord of Spirits, and confess their sins before Him. And they shall bless and glorify the Lord of Spirits, and say: 'Blessed is the Lord of Spirits and the Lord of kings, And the Lord of the mighty and the Lord of the rich, And the Lord of glory and the Lord of wisdom, 3 And splendid in every secret thing is Thy power from generation to generation, And Thy glory for ever and ever: Deep are all Thy secrets and innumerable, And Thy righteousness is beyond reckoning. 4 We have now learnt that we should glorify And bless the Lord of kings and Him who is king over all kings.' 5 And they shall say: 'Would that we had rest to glorify and give thanks And confess our faith before His glory! And now we long for a little rest but find it not: We follow hard upon and obtain (it) not: And light has vanished from before us, And darkness is our dwelling-place for ever and ever: 7 For we have not believed before Him Nor glorified the name of the Lord of Spirits, [nor glorified our Lord] But our hope was in the sceptre of our kingdom, And in our glory. 8 And in the day of our suffering and tribulation He saves us not, And we find no respite for confession That our Lord is true in all His works, and in His judgements and His justice, And His judgements have no respect of persons. 9 And we pass away from before His face on account of our works, And all our sins are reckoned up in righteousness.' 10 Now they shall say unto themselves: 'Our souls are full of unrighteous gain, but it does not prevent us from descending from the midst thereof into the burden of Sheol.' 11 And after that their faces shall be filled with darkness And shame before that Son of Man, And they shall be driven from his presence, And the sword shall abide before his face in their midst. 12 Thus spake the Lord of Spirits: 'This is the ordinance and judgement with respect to the mighty and the kings and the exalted and those who possess the earth before the Lord of Spirits.'

64 1, 2 And other forms I saw hidden in that place. I heard the voice of the angel saying: 'These are the angels who descended to the earth, and revealed what was hidden to the children of men and seduced the children of men into committing sin.'

65 1, 2 And in those days Noah saw the earth that it had sunk down and its destruction was nigh. And he arose from thence and went to the ends of the earth, and cried aloud to his grandfather Enoch: 3 and Noah said three times with an embittered voice: 'Hear me, hear me, hear me.' And I said unto him: 'Tell me what it is that is falling out on the earth that the earth is in such evil plight 4 and shaken, lest perchance I shall perish with it?' And thereupon there was a great commotion 5 on the earth, and a voice was heard from heaven, and I fell on my face. And Enoch my grandfather came and stood by me, and said unto me: 'Why hast thou cried unto me with a bitter cry and weeping? 6 And a command has gone forth from the presence of the Lord concerning those who dwell on the earth that their ruin is accomplished because they have learnt all the secrets of the angels, and all 6 And a command has gone forth from the presence of the Lord concerning those who dwell on the earth that their ruin is accomplished because they have learnt all the secrets of the angels, and all the violence of .the Satans, and all their powers the most secret one -- and all the power of those who practice sorcery, and the power of witchcraft, and the power of those who make molten images 7 for the whole earth: And how silver is produced from the dust of the earth, and how soft metal 8 originates in the earth. For lead and tin are not produced from the earth like the first: it is a fountain 9 that produces them, and an angel stands therein, and that angel is pre-eminent.' And after that my grandfather Enoch took hold of me by my hand and raised me up, and said unto me: 'Go, for I have 10 asked the Lord of Spirits as touching this commotion on the earth. And He said unto me: "Because of their unrighteousness their judgement has been determined upon and shall not be withheld by Me for ever. Because of the sorceries which they have searched out and learnt, the earth and those 11 who dwell upon it shall be destroyed." And these -- they have no place of repentance for ever, because they have shown them what was hidden, and they are the damned: but as for thee, my son, the Lord of Spirits knows that thou art pure, and guiltless of this reproach concerning the secrets. 12 And He has destined thy name to be among the holy, And will preserve thee amongst those who dwell on the earth, And has destined thy righteous seed both for kingship and for great honours, And from thy seed shall proceed a fountain of the righteous and holy without number for ever.'

66 1 And after that he showed me the angels of punishment who are prepared to come and let loose all the powers of the waters which are beneath in the earth in order to bring judgement and destruction 2 on all who [abide and] dwell on the earth. And the Lord of Spirits gave commandment to the angels who were going forth, that they should not cause the waters to rise but should hold them 3 in check; for those angels were over the powers of the waters. And I went away from the presence of Enoch.

67 1 And in those days the word of God came unto me, and He said unto me: 'Noah, thy lot has come 2 up before Me, a lot without blame, a lot of love and uprightness. And now the angels are making a wooden (building), and when they have completed that task I will place My hand upon it and preserve it, and there shall come forth from it the seed of life, and a change shall set in so that the 3 earth will not remain without inhabitant. And I will make fast thy seed before me for ever and ever, and I will spread abroad those who dwell with thee: it shall not be unfruitful on the face of the earth, but it shall be blessed and multiply on the earth in the name of the Lord.' 4 And He will imprison those angels, who have shown unrighteousness, in that burning valley which my grandfather Enoch had formerly shown to me in the west among the mountains of gold 5 and silver and iron and soft metal and tin. And I saw that valley in which there was a great 6 convulsion and a convulsion of the waters. And when all this took place, from that fiery molten metal and from the convulsion thereof in that place, there was produced a smell of sulphur, and it was connected with those waters, and that valley of the angels who had led astray (mankind) burned 7 beneath that land. And through its valleys proceed streams of fire, where these angels are punished who had led astray those who dwell upon the earth. 8 But those waters shall in those days serve for the kings and the mighty and the exalted, and those who dwell on the earth, for the healing of the body, but for the punishment of the spirit; now their spirit is full of lust, that they may be punished in their body, for they have denied the Lord of Spirits 9 and see their punishment daily, and yet believe not in His name. And in proportion as the burning of their bodies becomes severe, a corresponding change shall take place in their spirit for ever and ever; 10 for before the Lord of Spirits none shall utter an idle word. For the judgement shall come upon them, 11 because they believe in the lust of their body and deny the Spirit of the Lord. And those same waters will undergo a change in those days; for when those angels are punished in these waters, these watersprings shall change their temperature, and when the angels ascend, this water of the 12 springs shall change and become cold. And I heard Michael answering and saying: 'This judgement wherewith the angels are judged is a testimony for the kings and the mighty who possess the 13 earth.'Because these waters of judgement minister to the healing of the body of the kings and the lust of their body; therefore they will not see and will not believe that those waters will change and become a fire which burns for ever.

68 1 And after that my grandfather Enoch gave me the teaching of all the secrets in the book in the Parables which had been given to him, and he put them together for me in the words of the book 2 of the Parables. And on that day Michael answered Raphael and said: 'The power of the spirit transports and makes me to tremble because of the severity of the judgement of the secrets, the judgement of the angels: who can endure the severe judgement which has been executed, and before 3 which they melt away? 'And Michael answered again, and said to Raphael: 'Who is he whose heart is not softened concerning it, and whose reins are not troubled by this word of judgeMent 4 (that) has gone forth upon them because of those who have thus led them out? 'And it came to pass when he stood before the Lord of Spirits, Michael said thus to Raphael: 'I will not take their part under the eye of the Lord; for the Lord of Spirits has been angry with them because they do 5 as if they were the Lord. Therefore all that is hidden shall come upon them for ever and ever; for neither angel nor man shall have his portion (in it), but alone they have received their judgement for ever and ever.'

69 1 And after this judgement they shall terrify and make them to tremble because they have shown this to those who dwell on the earth. 2 And behold the names of those angels [and these are their names: the first of them is Samjaza, the second Artaqifa, and the third Armen, the fourth Kokabel, the fifth Turael, the sixth Rumjal, the seventh Danjal, the eighth Neqael, the ninth Baraqel, the tenth Azazel, the eleventh Armaros, the twelfth Batarjal, the thirteenth Busasejal, the fourteenth Hananel, the fifteenth Turel, and the sixteenth Simapesiel, the seventeenth Jetrel, the eighteenth Tumael, the nineteenth Turel, 3 the twentieth Rumael the twenty-first Azazel. And these are the chiefs of their angels and their names, and their chief ones over hundreds and over fifties and over tens]. 4 The name of the first Jeqon: that is, the one who led astray [all] the sons of God, and brought them 5 down to the earth, and led them astray through the daughters of men. And the second was named Asbeel: he imparted to the holy sons of God evil counsel, and led them astray so that they defiled 6 their bodies with the daughters of men. And the third was named Gadreel: he it is who showed the children off men all the blows of death, and he led astray Eve, and showed [the weapons of death to the sons of men] the shield and the coat of mail, and the sword for battle, and all the weapons 7 of death to the children of men. And from his hand they have proceeded against those who dwell 8 on the earth from that day and for evermore. And the fourth was named Penemue: he taught the 9 children of men the bitter and the sweet, and he taught them all the secrets of their wisdom. And he instructed mankind in writing with ink and paper, and thereby many sinned from eternity to 10 eternity and until this day. For men were not created for such a purpose, to give confirmation 11 to their good faith with pen and ink. For men were created exactly like the angels, to the intent that they should continue pure and righteous, and death, which destroys everything, could not have taken hold, of them, but through this their knowledge they are perishing, and through this power 12 it is consuming me. And the fifth was named Kasdeja: this is he who showed the children of men all the wicked smitings of spirits and demons, and the smitings of the embryo in the womb, that it may pass away, and [the smitings of the soul] the bites of the serpent, and the smitings 13 which befall through the noontide heat, the son of the serpent named Tabaet. And this is the task of Kasbeel, the chief of the oath which he showed to the holy ones when he dwelt high 14 above in glory, and its name is Biqa. This (angel) requested Michael to show him the hidden name that he might enunciate it in the oath, so that those might quake before that name and oath who 15 revealed all that was in secret to the children of men. And this is the power of this oath, for it is powerful and strong, and he placed this oath Akae in the hand of Michael. 16 And these are the secrets of this oath... And they are strong through his oath: And the heaven was suspended before the world was created, And for ever. 17 And through it the earth was founded upon the water, And from the secret recesses of the mountains come beautiful waters, From the creation of the world and unto eternity. 18 And through that oath the sea was created, And as its foundation He set for it the sand against the time of (its} anger, And it dare not pass beyond it from the creation of the world unto eternity. 19 And through that oath are the depths made fast, And abide and stir not from their place from eternity to eternity. 20 And through that oath the sun and moon complete their course, And deviate not from their ordinance from eternity to eternity. 21 And through that oath the stars complete their course, And He calls them by their names, And they answer Him from eternity to eternity. 22 [And in like manner the spirits of the water, and of the winds, and of all zephyrs, and (their) paths 23 from all the quarters of the winds. And there are preserved the voices of the thunder and the light of the lightnings: and there are preserved the chambers of the hail and the chambers of the hoar-frost, 24 and the chambers of the mist, and the chambers of the rain and the dew. And all these believe and give thanks before the Lord of Spirits, and glorify (Him) with all their power, and their food is in every act of thanksgiving: they thank and glorify and extol the name of the Lord of Spirits for ever and ever.] 25 And this oath is mighty over them, And through it [they are preserved and] their paths are preserved, And their course is not destroyed. 26 And there was great joy amongst them, And they blessed and glorified and extolled Because the name of that Son of Man had been revealed unto them. 27 And he sat on the throne of his glory, And the sum of judgement was given unto the Son of Man, And he caused the sinners to pass away and be destroyed from off the face of the earth, And those who have led the world astray. 28 With chains shall they be bound, And in their assemblage-place of destruction shall they be imprisoned, And all their works vanish from the face of the earth. 29 And from henceforth there shall be nothing corruptible; For that Son of Man has appeared, And has seated himself on the throne of his glory, And all evil shall pass away before his face, And the word of that Son of Man shall go forth And be strong before the Lord of Spirits. This is the third Parable of Enoch.

70 1 And it came to pass after this that his name during his lifetime was raised aloft to that Son of 2 Man and to the Lord of Spirits from amongst those who dwell on the earth. And he was raised aloft 3 on the chariots of the spirit and his name vanished among them. And from that day I was no longer numbered amongst them: and he set me between the two winds, between the North and the 4 West, where the angels took the cords to measure for me the place for the elect and righteous. And there I saw the first fathers and the righteous who from the beginning dwell in that place.

71 1 And it came to pass after this that my spirit was translated And it ascended into the heavens: And I saw the holy sons of God. They were stepping on flames of fire: Their garments were white [and their raiment], And their faces shone like snow. 2 And I saw two streams of fire; And the light of that fire shone like hyacinth, And I fell on my face before the Lord of Spirits. 3 And the angel Michael [one of the archangels] seized me by my right hand, And lifted me up and led me forth into all the secrets, And he showed me all the secrets of righteousness. 4 And he showed me all the secrets of the ends of the heaven, And all the chambers of all the stars, and all the luminaries, Whence they proceed before the face of the holy ones. 5 And he translated my spirit into the heaven of heavens, And I saw there as it were a structure built of crystals, And between those crystals tongues of living fire. 6 And my spirit saw the girdle which girt that house of fire, And on its four sides were streams full of living fire, And they girt that house. 7 And round about were Seraphin, Cherubin, and Ophannin: And these are they who sleep not And guard the throne of His glory. 8 And I saw angels who could not be counted, A thousand thousands, and ten thousand times ten thousand, Encircling that house. And Michael, and Raphael, and Gabriel, and Phanuel, And the holy angels who are above the heavens, Go in and out of that house. 9 And they came forth from that house, And Michael and Gabriel, Raphael and Phanuel, And many holy angels without number. 10 And with them the Head of Days, His head white and pure as wool, And His raiment indescribable. 11 And I fell on my face, And my whole body became relaxed, And my spirit was transfigured; And I cried with a loud voice, ...with the spirit of power, And blessed and glorified and extolled. 12 And these blessings which went forth out of my mouth were well pleasing before that Head of 13 Days. And that Head of Days came with Michael and Gabriel, Raphael and Phanuel, thousands and ten thousands of angels without number. [Lost passage wherein the Son of Man was described as accompanying the Head of Days, and Enoch asked one of the angels (as in xlvi 3) concerning the Son of Man as to who he was.] 14 And he (i.e. the angel) came to me and greeted me with His voice, and said unto me: 'This is the Son of Man who is born unto righteousness, And righteousness abides over him, And the righteousness of the Head of Days forsakes him not.' 15 And he said unto me: 'He proclaims unto thee peace in the name of the world to come; For from hence has proceeded peace since the creation of the world, And so shall it be unto thee for ever and for ever and ever. 16 And all shall walk in his ways since righteousness never forsaketh him: With him will be their dwelling-places, and with him their heritage, And they shall not be separated from him for ever and ever and ever. 17 And so there shall be length of days with that Son of Man, And the righteous shall have peace and an upright way In the name of the Lord of Spirits for ever and ever.'

72 1 The book of the courses of the luminaries of the heaven, the relations of each, according to their classes, their dominion and their seasons, according to their names and places of origin, and according to their months, which Uriel, the holy angel, who was with me, who is their guide, showed me; and he showed me all their laws exactly as they are, and how it is with regard to all the years of the world 2 and unto eternity, till the new creation is accomplished which dureth till eternity. And this is the first law of the luminaries: the luminary the Sun has its rising in the eastern portals of the heaven, 3 and its setting in the western portals of the heaven. And I saw six portals in which the sun rises, and six portals in which the sun sets: and the moon rises and sets in these portals, and the leaders of the stars and those whom they lead: six in the east and six in the west, and all following each other 4 in accurately corresponding order: also many windows to the right and left of these portals. And first there goes forth the great luminary, named the Sun, and his circumference is like the circumference 5 of the heaven, and he is quite filled with illuminating and heating fire. The chariot on which he ascends, the wind drives, and the sun goes down from the heaven and returns through the north in order to reach the east, and is so guided that he comes to the appropriate (lit. 'that') portal and 6 shines in the face of the heaven. In this way he rises in the first month in the great portal, which 7 is the fourth [those six portals in the east]. And in that fourth portal from which the sun rises in the first month are twelve window-openings, from which proceed a flame when they are opened in 8 their season. When the sun rises in the heaven, he comes forth through that fourth portal thirty 9 mornings in succession, and sets accurately in the fourth portal] in the west of the heaven. And during this period the day becomes daily longer and the night nightly shorter to the thirtieth 10 morning. On that day the day is longer than the night by a ninth part, and the day amounts exactly 11 to ten parts and the night to eight parts. And the sun rises from that fourth portal, and sets in the fourth and returns to the fifth portal of the east thirty mornings, and rises from it and sets in the fifth 12 portal. And then the day becomes longer by two parts and amounts to eleven parts, and the night 13 becomes shorter and amounts to seven parts. And it returns to the east and enters into the sixth 14 portal, and rises and sets in the sixth portal one-and-thirty mornings on account of its sign. On that day the day becomes longer than the night, and the day becomes double the night, and the day 15 becomes twelve parts, and the night is shortened and becomes six parts. And the sun mounts up to make the day shorter and the night longer, and the sun returns to the east and enters into the 16 sixth portal, and rises from it and sets thirty mornings. And when thirty mornings are accomplished, 17 the day decreases by exactly one part, and becomes eleven parts and the night seven. And the sun goes forth from that sixth portal in the west, and goes to the east and rises in the fifth portal for thirty 18 mornings, and sets in the west again in the fifth western portal. On that day the day decreases 19 by two parts, and amounts to ten parts and the night to eight parts. And the sun goes forth from that fifth portal and sets in the fifth portal of the west, and rises in the fourth portal for 20 one-and-thirty mornings on account of its sign, and sets in the west. On that day the day is equalized with the night, [and becomes of equal length], and the night amounts to nine parts and the day to 21 nine parts. And the sun rises from that portal and sets in the west, and returns to the east and rises 22 thirty mornings in the third portal and sets in the west in the third portal. And on that day the night becomes longer than the day, and night becomes longer than night, and day shorter than day till the thirtieth morning; and the night amounts exactly to ten parts and the day to eight 23 parts. And the sun rises from that third portal and sets in the third portal in the west and returns to the east, and for thirty mornings rises m the second portal in the east, and in like manner sets 24 in the second portal in the west of the heaven. And on that day the night amounts to eleven 25 parts and the day to seven parts. And the sun rises on that day from that second portal and sets in the west in the second portal, and returns to the east into the first portal for one-and -thirty 26 mornings, and sets in the first portal in the west of the heaven. And on that day the night becomes longer and amounts to the double of the day: and the night amounts exactly to twelve parts and 27 the day to six. And the sun has (therewith) traversed the divisions of his orbit and turns again on those divisions of his orbit, and enters that portal thirty mornings and sets also in the west 28 opposite to it. And on that night has the night decreased in length by a ninth part, and the night 29 has become eleven parts and the day seven parts. And the sun has returned and entered into the second portal in the east, and returns on those his divisions of his orbit for thirty mornings, rising 30 and setting. And on that day the night decreases in length, and the night amounts to ten parts 31 and the day to eight. And on that day the sun rises from that portal, and sets in the west, and returns to the east, and rises in the third portal for one-and-thirty mornings, and sets in the west of the heaven. 32 On that day the night decreases and amounts to nine parts, and the day to nine parts, and the night 33 is equal to the day and the year is exactly as to its days three hundred and sixty-four. And the length of the day and of the night, and the shortness of the day and of the night arise --through the course 34 of the sun these distinctions are made (lit. 'they are separated'). So it comes that its course becomes 35 daily longer, and its course nightly shorter. And this is the law and the course of the sun, and his return as often as he returns sixty times and rises, ie, the great luminary which is named the sun, 36 for ever and ever. And that which (thus) rises is the great luminary, and is so named according to 37 its appearance, according as the Lord commanded. As he rises, so he sets and decreases not, and rests not, but runs day and night, and his light is sevenfold brighter than that of the moon; but as regards size they are both equal.

73 1 And after this law I saw another law dealing with the smaller luminary, which is named the Moon. 2 And her circumference is like the circumference of the heaven, and her chariot in which she rides 3 is driven by the wind, and light is given to her in (definite) measure. And her rising and setting change every month: and her days are like the days of the sun, and when her light is uniform 4 (i.e. full) it amounts to the seventh part of the light of the sun. And thus she rises. And her first phase in the east comes forth on the thirtieth morning: and on that day she becomes visible, and constitutes for you the first phase of the moon on the thirtieth day together with the sun in the 5 portal where the sun rises. And the one half of her goes forth by a seventh part, and her whole circumference is empty, without light, with the exception of one-seventh part of it, (and) the fourteenth 6 part of her light. And when she receives one-seventh part of the half of her light, her light 7 amounts to one-seventh part and the half thereof. And she sets with the sun, and when the sun rises the moon rises with him and receives the half of one part of light, and in that night in the beginning of her morning [in the commencement of the lunar day] the moon sets with the sun, and 8 is invisible that night with the fourteen parts and the half of one of them. And she rises on that day with exactly a seventh part, and comes forth and recedes from the rising of the sun, and in her remaining days she becomes bright in the (remaining) thirteen parts.

74 1 And I saw another course, a law for her, (and) how according to that law she performs her monthly 2 revolution. And all these Uriel, the holy angel who is the leader of them all, showed to me, and their positions, and I wrote down their positions as he showed them to me, and I wrote down their months 3 as they were, and the appearance of their lights till fifteen days were accomplished. In single seventh parts she accomplishes all her light in the east, and in single seventh parts accomplishes all her 4 darkness in the west. And in certain months she alters her settings, and in certain months she pursues 5 her own peculiar course. In two months the moon sets with the sun: in those two middle portals the 6 third and the fourth. She goes forth for seven days, and turns about and returns again through the portal where the sun rises, and accomplishes all her light: and she recedes from the sun, and in eight 7 days enters the sixth portal from which the sun goes forth. And when the sun goes forth from the fourth portal she goes forth seven days, until she goes forth from the fifth and turns back again in seven days into the fourth portal and accomplishes all her light: and she recedes and enters into the 8 first portal in eight days. And she returns again in seven days into the fourth portal from which the 9, 10 sun goes forth, Thus I saw their position -- how the moons rose and the sun set in those days. And if five years are added together the sun has an overplus of thirty days, and all the days which accrue 11 to it for one of those five years, when they are full, amount to 364 days. And the overplus of the sun and of the stars amounts to six days: in 5 years 6 days every year come to 30 days: and the 12 moon falls behind the sun and stars to the number of 30 days. And the sun and the stars bring in all the years exactly, so that they do not advance or delay their position by a single day unto eternity; 13 but complete the years with perfect justice in 364 days. In 3 years there are 1,092 days, and in 14 5 years 1,820 days, so that in 8 years there are 2,912 days. For the moon alone the days amount in 3 years to 1,062 days, and in 5 years she falls 50 days behind: [i.e. to the sum (of 1,770) there is 15 to be added (1,000 and) 62 days.] And in 5 years there are 1,770 days, so that for the moon the days 16 in 8 years amount to 2,832 days. [For in 8 years she falls behind to the amount of 80 days], all the 17 days she falls behind in 8 years are 80. And the year is accurately completed in conformity with their world-stations and the stations of the sun, which rise from the portals through which it (the sun) rises and sets 30 days.

75 1 And the leaders of the heads of the thousands, who are placed over the whole creation and over all the stars, have also to do with the four intercalary days, being inseparable from their office, according to the reckoning of the year, and these render service on the four days which are not 2 reckoned in the reckoning of the year. And owing to them men go wrong therein, for those luminaries truly render service on the world-stations, one in the first portal, one in the third portal of the heaven, one in the fourth portal, and one in the sixth portal, and the exactness of the year is 3 accomplished through its separate three hundred and sixty-four stations. For the signs and the times and the years and the days the angel Uriel showed to me, whom the Lord of glory hath set for ever over all the luminaries of the heaven, in the heaven and in the world, that they should rule on the face of the heaven and be seen on the earth, and be leaders for the day and the night, i.e. the sun, moon, and stars, and all the ministering creatures which make their revolution in all the chariots 4 of the heaven. In like manner twelve doors Uriel showed me, open in the circumference of the sun's chariot in the heaven, through which the rays of the sun break forth: and from them is warmth 5 diffused over the earth, when they are opened at their appointed seasons. [And for the winds and 6 the spirit of the dew when they are opened, standing open in the heavens at the ends.] As for the twelve portals in the heaven, at the ends of the earth, out of which go forth the sun, moon, and stars, 7 and all the works of heaven in the east and in the west, There are many windows open to the left and right of them, and one window at its (appointed) season produces warmth, corresponding (as these do) to those doors from which the stars come forth according as He has commanded them, 8 and wherein they set corresponding to their number. And I saw chariots in the heaven, running 9 in the world, above those portals in which revolve the stars that never set. And one is larger than all the rest, and it is that that makes its course through the entire world.

76 1 And at the ends of the earth I saw twelve portals open to all the quarters (of the heaven), from 2 which the winds go forth and blow over the earth. Three of them are open on the face (i.e. the east) of the heavens, and three in the west, and three on the right (i.e. the south) of the heaven, and 3 three on the left (i.e. the north). And the three first are those of the east, and three are of the 4 north, and three [after those on the left] of the south, and three of the west. Through four of these come winds of blessing and prosperity, and from those eight come hurtful winds: when they are sent, they bring destruction on all the earth and on the water upon it, and on all who dwell thereon, and on everything which is in the water and on the land. 5 And the first wind from those portals, called the east wind, comes forth through the first portal which is in the east, inclining towards the south: from it come forth desolation, drought, heat, 6 and destruction. And through the second portal in the middle comes what is fitting, and from it there come rain and fruitfulness and prosperity and dew; and through the third portal which lies toward the north come cold and drought. 7 And after these come forth the south winds through three portals: through the first portal of 8 them inclining to the east comes forth a hot wind. And through the middle portal next to it there 9 come forth fragrant smells, and dew and rain, and prosperity and health. And through the third portal lying to the west come forth dew and rain, locusts and desolation. 10 And after these the north winds: from the seventh portal in the east come dew and rain, locusts 11 and desolation. And from the middle portal come in a direct direction health and rain and dew and prosperity; and through the third portal in the west come cloud and hoar-frost, and snow and rain, and dew and locusts. 12 And after these [four] are the west winds: through the first portal adjoining the north come forth 13 dew and hoar-frost, and cold and snow and frost. And from the middle portal come forth dew and rain, and prosperity and blessing; and through the last portal which adjoins the south come forth 14 drought and desolation, and burning and destruction. And the twelve portals of the four quarters of the heaven are therewith completed, and all their laws and all their plagues and all their benefactions have I shown to thee, my son Methuselah.

77 1 And the first quarter is called the east, because it is the first: and the second, the south, because the Most High will descend there, yea, there in quite a special sense will He who is blessed for ever 2 descend. And the west quarter is named the diminished, because there all the luminaries of the 3 heaven wane and go down. And the fourth quarter, named the north, is divided into three parts: the first of them is for the dwelling of men: and the second contains seas of water, and the abysses and forests and rivers, and darkness and clouds; and the third part contains the garden of righteousness. 4 I saw seven high mountains, higher than all the mountains which are on the earth: and thence 5 comes forth hoar-frost, and days, seasons, and years pass away. I saw seven rivers on the earth larger than all the rivers: one of them coming from the west pours its waters into the Great Sea. 6 And these two come from the north to the sea and pour their waters into the Erythraean Sea in the 7 east. And the remaining four come forth on the side of the north to their own sea, (two of them to) the Erythraean Sea, and two into the Great Sea and discharge themselves there [and some say: 8 into the desert]. Seven great islands I saw in the sea and in the mainland: two in the mainland and five in the Great Sea.

78 1,2 And the names of the sun are the following: the first Orjares, and the second Tomas. And the moon has four names: the first name is Asonja, the second Ebla, the third Benase, and the fourth 3 Erae. These are the two great luminaries: their circumference is like the circumference of the 4 heaven, and the size of the circumference of both is alike. In the circumference of the sun there are seven portions of light which are added to it more than to the moon, and in definite measures it is 5 transferred till the seventh portion of the sun is exhausted. And they set and enter the portals of the west, and make their revolution by the north, and come forth through the eastern portals 6 on the face of the heaven. And when the moon rises one-fourteenth part appears in the heaven: 7 [the light becomes full in her]: on the fourteenth day she accomplishes her light. And fifteen parts of light are transferred to her till the fifteenth day (when) her light is accomplished, according to the sign of the year, and she becomes fifteen parts, and the moon grows by (the addition of) fourteenth 8 parts. And in her waning (the moon) decreases on the first day to fourteen parts of her light, on the second to thirteen parts of light, on the third to twelve, on the fourth to eleven, on the fifth to ten, on the sixth to nine, on the seventh to eight, on the eighth to seven, on the ninth to six, on the tenth to five, on the eleventh to four, on the twelfth to three, on the thirteenth to two, on the fourteenth 9 to the half of a seventh, and all her remaining light disappears wholly on the fifteenth. And 10 in certain months the month has twenty-nine days and once twenty-eight. And Uriel showed me another law: when light is transferred to the moon, and on which side it is transferred to her by 11 the sun. During all the period during which the moon is growing in her light, she is transferring it to herself when opposite to the sun during fourteen days [her light is accomplished in the heaven], 12 and when she is illumined throughout, her light is accomplished full in the heaven. And on the first 13 day she is called the new moon, for on that day the light rises upon her. She becomes full moon exactly on the day when the sun sets in the west, and from the east she rises at night, and the moon shines the whole night through till the sun rises over against her and the moon is seen over against 14 the sun. On the side whence the light of the moon comes forth, there again she wanes till all the light vanishes and all the days of the month are at an end, and her circumference is empty, void of 15 light. And three months she makes of thirty days, and at her time she makes three months of twenty-nine days each, in which she accomplishes her waning in the first period of time, and in the first 16 portal for one hundred and seventy-seven days. And in the time of her going out she appears for 17 three months (of) thirty days each, and for three months she appears (of) twenty-nine each. At night she appears like a man for twenty days each time, and by day she appears like the heaven, and there is nothing else in her save her light.

79 1 And now, my son, I have shown thee everything, and the law of all the stars of the heaven is 2 completed. And he showed me all the laws of these for every day, and for every season of bearing rule, and for every year, and for its going forth, and for the order prescribed to it every month 3 and every week: And the waning of the moon which takes place in the sixth portal: for in this 4 sixth portal her light is accomplished, and after that there is the beginning of the waning: (And the waning) which takes place in the first portal in its season, till one hundred and seventy -seven 5 days are accomplished: reckoned according to weeks, twenty-five (weeks) and two days. She falls behind the sun and the order of the stars exactly five days m the course of one period, and when 6 this place which thou seest has been traversed. Such is the picture and sketch of every luminary which Uriel the archangel, who is their leader, showed unto me.

80 1 And in those days the angel Uriel answered and said to me: 'Behold, I have shown thee everything, Enoch, and I have revealed everything to thee that thou shouldst see this sun and this moon, and the leaders of the stars of the heaven and all those who turn them, their tasks and times and departures. 2 And in the days of the sinners the years shall be shortened, And their seed shall be tardy on their lands and fields, And all things on the earth shall alter, And shall not appear in their time: And the rain shall be kept back And the heaven shall withhold (it). 3 And in those times the fruits of the earth shall be backward, And shall not grow in their time, And the fruits of the trees shall be withheld in their time. 4 And the moon shall alter her order, And not appear at her time. 5 [And in those days the sun shall be seen and he shall journey in the evening on the extremity of the great chariot in the west] And shall shine more brightly than accords with the order of light. 6 And many chiefs of the stars shall transgress the order (prescribed). And these shall alter their orbits and tasks, And not appear at the seasons prescribed to them. 7 And the whole order of the stars shall be concealed from the sinners, And the thoughts of those on the earth shall err concerning them, [And they shall be altered from all their ways], Yea, they shall err and take them to be gods. 8 And evil shall be multiplied upon them, And punishment shall come upon them So as to destroy all.'

81 1 And he said unto me: 'Observe, Enoch, these heavenly tablets, And read what is written thereon, And mark every individual fact.' 2 And I observed the heavenly tablets, and read everything which was written (thereon) and understood everything, and read the book of all the deeds of mankind, and of all the children of flesh 3 that shall be upon the earth to the remotest generations. And forthwith I blessed the great Lord the King of glory for ever, in that He has made all the works of the world, And I extolled the Lord because of His patience, And blessed Him because of the children of men. 4 And after that I said: 'Blessed is the man who dies in righteousness and goodness, Concerning whom there is no book of unrighteousness written, And against whom no day of judgement shall be found.' 5 And those seven holy ones brought me and placed me on the earth before the door of my house, and said to me: 'Declare everything to thy son Methuselah, and show to all thy children that no 6 flesh is righteous in the sight of the Lord, for He is their Creator. One year we will leave thee with thy son, till thou givest thy (last) commands, that thou mayst teach thy children and record (it) for them, and testify to all thy children; and in the second year they shall take thee from their midst. 7 Let thy heart be strong, For the good shall announce righteousness to the good; The righteous with the righteous shall rejoice, And shall offer congratulation to one another. 8 But the sinners shall die with the sinners, And the apostate go down with the apostate. 9 And those who practice righteousness shall die on account of the deeds of men, And be taken away on account of the doings of the godless.' 10 And in those days they ceased to speak to me, and I came to my people, blessing the Lord of the world.

82 1 And now, my son Methuselah, all these things I am recounting to thee and writing down for thee, and I have revealed to thee everything, and given thee books concerning all these: so preserve, my son Methuselah, the books from thy father's hand, and (see) that thou deliver them to the generations of the world. 2 I have given wisdom to thee and to thy children, [And thy children that shall be to thee], That they may give it to their children for generations, This wisdom (namely) that passeth their thought. 3 And those who understand it shall not sleep, But shall listen with the ear that they may learn this wisdom, And it shall please those that eat thereof better than good food. 4 Blessed are all the righteous, blessed are all those who walk in the way of righteousness and sin not as the sinners, in the reckoning of all their days in which the sun traverses the heaven, entering into and departing from the portals for thirty days with the heads of thousands of the order of the stars, together with the four which are intercalated which divide the four portions of the year, which 5 lead them and enter with them four days. Owing to them men shall be at fault and not reckon them in the whole reckoning of the year: yea, men shall be at fault, and not recognize them accurately. 6 For they belong to the reckoning of the year and are truly recorded (thereon) for ever, one in the first portal and one in the third, and one in the fourth and one in the sixth, and the year is completed in three hundred and sixty-four days. 7 And the account thereof is accurate and the recorded reckoning thereof exact; for the luminaries, and months and festivals, and years and days, has Uriel shown and revealed to me, to whom the 8 Lord of the whole creation of the world hath subjected the host of heaven. And he has power over night and day in the heaven to cause the light to give light to men sun, moon, and stars, 9 and all the powers of the heaven which revolve in their circular chariots. And these are the orders of the stars, which set in their places, and in their seasons and festivals and months. 10 And these are the names of those who lead them, who watch that they enter at their times, in their orders, in their seasons, in their months, in their periods of dominion, and in their positions. 11 Their four leaders who divide the four parts of the year enter first; and after them the twelve leaders of the orders who divide the months; and for the three hundred and sixty (days) there are heads over thousands who divide the days; and for the four intercalary days there are the leaders which sunder 12 the four parts of the year. And these heads over thousands are intercalated between leader and 13 leader, each behind a station, but their leaders make the division. And these are the names of the leaders who divide the four parts of the year which are ordained: Milkiel, Hel 'emmelek, and Mel'ejal, 14 and Narel. And the names of those who lead them: Adnar'el, and Ijasusa'el, and 'Elome'el these three follow the leaders of the orders, and there is one that follows the three leaders of the orders which follow those leaders of stations that divide the four parts of the year. 15 In the beginning of the year Melkejal rises first and rules, who is named Tam'aini and sun, and 16 all the days of his dominion whilst he bears rule are ninety-one days. Arid these are the signs of the days which are to be seen on earth in the days of his dominion: sweat, and heat, and calms; and all the trees bear fruit, and leaves are produced on all the trees, and the harvest of wheat, and the rose-flowers, and all the flowers which come forth in the field, but the trees of the winter season 17 become withered. And these are the names of the leaders which are under them: Berka'el, Zelebs'el, and another who is added a head of a thousand, called Hilujaseph: and the days of the dominion of this (leader) are at an end. 18 The next leader after him is Hel'emmelek, whom one names the shining sun, and all the days 19 of his light are ninety-one days. And these are the signs of (his) days on the earth: glowing heat and dryness, and the trees ripen their fruits and produce all their fruits ripe and ready, and the sheep pair and become pregnant, and all the fruits of the earth are gathered in, and everything that is 20 in the fields, and the winepress: these things take place in the days of his dominion. These are the names, and the orders, and the leaders of those heads of thousands: Gida'ijal, Ke'el, and He'el, and the name of the head of a thousand which is added to them, Asfa'el: and the days of his dominion are at an end.

83 1 And now, my son Methuselah, I will show thee all my visions which I have seen, recounting 2 them before thee. Two visions I saw before I took a wife, and the one was quite unlike the other: the first when I was learning to write: the second before I took thy mother, (when) I saw a terrible

3 vision. And regarding them I prayed to the Lord. I had laid me down in the house of my grandfather Mahalalel, (when) I saw in a vision how the heaven collapsed and was borne off and fell to 4 the earth. And when it fell to the earth I saw how the earth was swallowed up in a great abyss, and mountains were suspended on mountains, and hills sank down on hills, and high trees were rent 5 from their stems, and hurled down and sunk in the abyss. And thereupon a word fell into my mouth, 6 and I lifted up (my voice) to cry aloud, and said: 'The earth is destroyed.' And my grandfather Mahalalel waked me as I lay near him, and said unto me: 'Why dost thou cry so, my son, and why 7 dost thou make such lamentation? 'And I recounted to him the whole vision which I had seen, and he said unto me : 'A terrible thing hast thou seen, my son, and of grave moment is thy dream-vision as to the secrets of all the sin of the earth: it must sink into the abyss and be destroyed with 8 a great destruction. And now, my son, arise and make petition to the Lord of glory, since thou art a believer, that a remnant may remain on the earth, and that He may not destroy the whole 9 earth. My son, from heaven all this will come upon the earth, and upon the earth there will be great 10 destruction. After that I arose and prayed and implored and besought, and wrote down my prayer 11 for the generations of the world, and I will show everything to thee, my son Methuselah. And when I had gone forth below and seen the heaven, and the sun rising in the east, and the moon setting in the west, and a few stars, and the whole earth, and everything as He had known it in the beginning, then I blessed the Lord of judgement and extolled Him because He had made the sun to go forth from the windows of the east, and he ascended and rose on the face of the heaven, and set out and kept traversing the path shown unto him.

84 1 And I lifted up my hands in righteousness and blessed the Holy and Great One, and spake with the breath of my mouth, and with the tongue of flesh, which God has made for the children of the flesh of men, that they should speak therewith, and He gave them breath and a tongue and a mouth that they should speak therewith: 2 'Blessed be Thou, O Lord, King, Great and mighty in Thy greatness, Lord of the whole creation of the heaven, King of kings and God of the whole world. And Thy power and kingship and greatness abide for ever and ever, And throughout all generations Thy dominion; And all the heavens are Thy throne for ever, And the whole earth Thy footstool for ever and ever. 3 For Thou hast made and Thou rulest all things, And nothing is too hard for Thee, Wisdom departs not from the place of Thy throne, Nor turns away from Thy presence. And Thou knowest and seest and hearest everything, And there is nothing hidden from Thee [for Thou seest everything]. 4 And now the angels of Thy heavens are guilty of trespass, And upon the flesh of men abideth Thy wrath until the great day of judgement. 5 And now, O God and Lord and Great King, I implore and beseech Thee to fulfil my prayer, To leave me a posterity on earth, And not destroy all the flesh of man, And make the earth without inhabitant, So that there should be an eternal destruction. 6 And now, my Lord, destroy from the earth the flesh which has aroused Thy wrath, But the flesh of righteousness and uprightness establish as a plant of the eternal seed, And hide not Thy face from the prayer of Thy servant, O Lord.'

85 1, 2 And after this I saw another dream, and I will show the whole dream to thee, my son. And Enoch lifted up (his voice) and spoke to his son Methuselah: 'To thee, my son, will I speak: hear my 3 words -incline thine ear to the dream-vision of thy father. Before I took thy mother Edna, I saw in a vision on my bed, and behold a bull came forth from the earth, and that bull was white; and after it came forth a heifer, and along with this (latter) came forth two bulls, one of them black and 4 the other red. And that black bull gored the red one and pursued him over the earth, and thereupon 5 I could no longer see that red bull. But that black bull grew and that heifer went with him, and 6 I saw that many oxen proceeded from him which resembled and followed him. And that cow, that first one, went from the presence of that first bull in order to seek that red one, but found him 7 not, and lamented with a great lamentation over him and sought him. And I looked till that first 8 bull came to her and quieted her, and from that time onward she cried no more. And after that she bore another white bull, and after him she bore many bulls and black cows. 9 And I saw in my sleep that white bull likewise grow and become a great white bull, and from him 10 proceeded many white bulls, and they resembled him. And they began to beget many white bulls, which resembled them, one following the other, (even) many.

86 1 And again I saw with mine eyes as I slept, and I saw the heaven above, and behold a star fell 2 from heaven, and it arose and eat and pastured amongst those oxen. And after that I saw the large and the black oxen, and behold they all changed their stalls and pastures and their cattle, and began 3 to live with each other. And again I saw in the vision, and looked towards the heaven, and behold I saw many stars descend and cast themselves down from heaven to that first star, and they became 4 bulls amongst those cattle and pastured with them [amongst them]. And I looked at them and saw, and behold they all let out their privy members, like horses, and began to cover the cows of the oxen, 5 and they all became pregnant and bare elephants, camels, and asses. And all the oxen feared them and were affrighted at them, and began to bite with their teeth and to devour, and to gore with their 6 horns. And they began, moreover, to devour those oxen; and behold all the children of the earth began to tremble and quake before them and to flee from them.'

87 1 And again I saw how they began to gore each other and to devour each other, and the earth 2 began to cry aloud. And I raised mine eyes again to heaven, and I saw in the vision, and behold there came forth from heaven beings who were like white men: and four went forth from that place 3 and three with them. And those three that had last come forth grasped me by my hand and took me up, away from the generations of the earth, and raised me up to a lofty place, and showed me 4 a tower raised high above the earth, and all the hills were lower. And one said unto me: 'Remain here till thou seest everything that befalls those elephants, camels, and asses, and the stars and the oxen, and all of them.'

88 1 And I saw one of those four who had come forth first, and he seized that first star which had fallen from the heaven, and bound it hand and foot and cast it into an abyss: now that abyss was 2 narrow and deep, and horrible and dark. And one of them drew a sword, and gave it to those elephants and camels and asses: then they began to smite each other, and the whole earth quaked 3 because of them. And as I was beholding in the vision, lo, one of those four who had come forth stoned. (them) from heaven, and gathered and took all the great stars whose privy members were like those of horses, and bound them all hand and foot, and cast them in an abyss of the earth.

89 1 And one of those four went to that white bull and instructed him in a secret, without his being terrified: he was born a bull and became a man, and built for himself a great vessel and dwelt thereon; 2 and three bulls dwelt with him in that vessel and they were covered in. And again I raised mine eyes towards heaven and saw a lofty roof, with seven water torrents thereon, and those torrents 3 flowed with much water into an enclosure. And I saw again, and behold fountains were opened on the surface of that great enclosure, and that water began to swell and rise upon the surface, 4 and I saw that enclosure till all its surface was covered with water. And the water, the darkness, and mist increased upon it; and as I looked at the height of that water, that water had risen above the height of that enclosure, and was streaming over that enclosure, and it stood upon the earth. 5 And all the cattle of that enclosure were gathered together until I saw how they sank and were 6 swallowed up and perished in that water. But that vessel floated on the water, while all the oxen and elephants and camels and asses sank to the bottom with all the animals, so that I could no longer 7 see them, and they were not able to escape, (but) perished and sank into the depths. And again I saw in the vision till those water torrents were removed from that high roof, and the chasms 8 of the earth were leveled up and other abysses were opened. Then the water began to run down into these, till the earth became visible; but that vessel settled on the earth, and the darkness 9 retired and light appeared. But that white bull which had become a man came out of that vessel, and the three bulls with him, and one of those three was white like that bull, and one of them was red as blood, and one black: and that white bull departed from them. 10 And they began to bring forth beasts of the field and birds, so that there arose different genera: lions, tigers, wolves, dogs, hyenas, wild boars, foxes, squirrels, swine, falcons, vultures, kites, 11 eagles, and ravens; and among them was born a white bull. And they began to bite one another; but that white bull which was born amongst them begat a wild ass and a white bull with it, and the 12 wild asses multiplied. But that bull which was born from him begat a black wild boar and a white 13 sheep; and the former begat many boars, but that sheep begat twelve sheep. And when those twelve sheep had grown, they gave up one of them to the asses, and those asses again gave up that sheep 14 to the wolves, and that sheep grew up among the wolves. And the Lord brought the eleven sheep to live with it and to pasture with it among the wolves: and they multiplied and became many 15 flocks of sheep. And the wolves began to fear them, and they oppressed them until they destroyed their little ones, and they cast their young into a river of much water: but those sheep began to 16 cry aloud on account of their little ones, and to complain unto their Lord. And a sheep which had been saved from the wolves fled and escaped to the wild asses; and I saw the sheep how they lamented and cried, and besought their Lord with all their might, till that Lord of the sheep descended 17 at the voice of the sheep from a lofty abode, and came to them and pastured them. And He called that sheep which had escaped the wolves, and spake with it concerning the wolves that it should 18 admonish them not to touch the sheep. And the sheep went to the wolves according to the word of the Lord, and another sheep met it and went with it, and the two went and entered together into the assembly of those wolves, and spake with them and admonished them not to touch the 19 sheep from henceforth. And thereupon I saw the wolves, and how they oppressed the sheep exceedingly 20 with all their power; and the sheep cried aloud. And the Lord came to the sheep and they began to smite those wolves: and the wolves began to make lamentation; but the sheep became 21 quiet and forthwith ceased to cry out. And I saw the sheep till they departed from amongst the wolves; but the eyes of the wolves were blinded, and those wolves departed in pursuit of the sheep

22 with all their power. And the Lord of the sheep went with them, as their leader, and all His sheep 23 followed Him: and His face was dazzling and glorious and terrible to behold. But the wolves 24 began to pursue those sheep till they reached a sea of water. And that sea was divided, and the water stood on this side and on that before their face, and their Lord led them and placed Himself between 25 them and the wolves. And as those wolves did not yet see the sheep, they proceeded into the midst of that sea, and the wolves followed the sheep, and [those wolves] ran after them into that sea. 26 And when they saw the Lord of the sheep, they turned to flee before His face, but that sea gathered itself together, and became as it had been created, and the water swelled and rose till it covered 27 those wolves. And I saw till all the wolves who pursued those sheep perished and were drowned. 28 But the sheep escaped from that water and went forth into a wilderness, where there was no water and no grass; and they began to open their eyes and to see; and I saw the Lord of the sheep 29 pasturing them and giving them water and grass, and that sheep going and leading them. And that 30 sheep ascended to the summit of that lofty rock, and the Lord of the sheep sent it to them. And after that I saw the Lord of the sheep who stood before them, and His appearance was great and 31 terrible and majestic, and all those sheep saw Him and were afraid before His face. And they all feared and trembled because of Him, and they cried to that sheep with them [which was amongst 32 them]: 'We are not able to stand before our Lord or to behold Him.' And that sheep which led them again ascended to the summit of that rock, but the sheep began to be blinded and to wander 33 from the way which he had showed them, but that sheep wot not thereof. And the Lord of the sheep was wrathful exceedingly against them, and that sheep discovered it, and went down

from the summit of the rock, and came to the sheep, and found the greatest part of them blinded and fallen 34 away. And when they saw it they feared and trembled at its presence, and desired to return to their 35 folds. And that sheep took other sheep with it, and came to those sheep which had fallen away, and began to slay them; and the sheep feared its presence, and thus that sheep brought back those 36 sheep that had fallen away, and they returned to their folds. And I saw in this vision till that sheep became a man and built a house for the Lord of the sheep, and placed all the sheep in that house. 37 And I saw till this sheep which had met that sheep which led them fell asleep: and I saw till all the great sheep perished and little ones arose in their place, and they came to a pasture, and 38 approached a stream of water. Then that sheep, their leader which had become a man, withdrew 39 from them and fell asleep, and all the sheep sought it and cried over it with a great crying. And I saw till they left off crying for that sheep and crossed that stream of water, and there arose the two sheep as leaders in the place of those which had led them and fallen asleep (lit. 'had fallen asleep and led 40 them'). And I saw till the sheep came to a goodly place, and a pleasant and glorious land, and I saw till those sheep were satisfied; and that house stood amongst them in the pleasant land. 41 And sometimes their eyes were opened, and sometimes blinded, till another sheep arose and led them and brought them all back, and their eyes were opened. 42 And the dogs and the foxes and the wild boars began to devour those sheep till the Lord of the sheep raised up [another sheep] a ram from their 43 midst, which led them. And that ram began to butt on either side those dogs, foxes, and wild 44 boars till he had destroyed them all. And that sheep whose eyes were opened saw that ram, which was amongst the sheep, till it forsook its glory and began to butt those sheep, and trampled upon them, and behaved itself 45 unseemly. And the Lord of the sheep sent the lamb to another lamb and raised it to being a ram and leader of the sheep instead of that 46 ram which had forsaken its glory. And it went to it and spake to it alone, and raised it to being a ram, and made it the prince and leader of the sheep; but during all these things those dogs 47 oppressed the sheep. And the first ram pursued that second ram, and that second ram arose and fled before it; and I saw till those dogs pulled 48 down the first ram. And that second ram arose 49 and led the [little] sheep. And those sheep grew and multiplied; but all the dogs, and foxes, and wild boars feared and fled before it, and that ram butted and killed the wild beasts, and those wild beasts had no longer any power among the 48b sheep and robbed them no more of ought. And that ram begat many sheep and fell asleep and 50 And that house became great and broad, and it was built for those sheep: and a tower lofty and great was built on the house for the Lord of the sheep, and that house was low but the tower was elevated and lofty, and the Lord of the sheep stood on that tower and they offered a full table before Him. 51 And again I saw those sheep that they again erred and went many ways, and forsook that their house, and the Lord of the sheep called some from amongst the sheep and sent them to the sheep, 52 but the sheep began to slay them. And one of them was saved and was not slain, and it sped away and cried aloud over the sheep; and they sought to slay it, but the Lord of the sheep saved it from 53 the sheep, and brought it up to me, and caused it to dwell there. And many other sheep He sent 54 to those sheep to testify unto them and lament over them. And after that I saw that when they forsook the house of the Lord and His tower they fell away entirely, and their eyes were blinded; and I saw the Lord of the sheep how He wrought much slaughter amongst them in their herds until 55 those sheep invited that slaughter and betrayed His place. And He gave them over into the hands of the lions and tigers, and wolves and hyenas, and into the hand of the foxes, and to all the wild 56 beasts, and those wild beasts began to tear in pieces those sheep. And I saw that He forsook that their house and their tower and gave them all into the hand of the lions, to tear and devour them, 57 into the hand of all the wild beasts. And I began to cry aloud with all my power, and to appeal to the Lord of the sheep, and to represent to Him in regard to the sheep that they were devoured 58 by all the wild beasts. But He remained unmoved, though He saw it, and rejoiced that they were devoured and swallowed and robbed, and left them to be devoured in the hand of all the beasts. 59 And He called seventy shepherds, and cast those sheep to them that they might pasture them, and He spake to the shepherds and their companions: 'Let each individual of you pasture the sheep 60 henceforward, and everything that I shall command you that do ye. And I will deliver them over unto you duly numbered, and tell you which of them are to be destroyed and them destroy ye.' And 61 He gave over unto them those sheep. And He called another and spake unto him: 'Observe and mark everything that the shepherds will do to those sheep; for they will destroy more of them than 62 I have commanded them. And every excess and the destruction which will be wrought through the shepherds, record (namely) how many they destroy according to my command, and how many according to their own caprice: record against every individual shepherd all the destruction he 63 effects. And read out before me by number how many they destroy, and how many they deliver over for destruction, that I may have this as a testimony against them, and know every deed of the shepherds, that I may comprehend and see what they do, whether or not they abide by my 64 command which I have commanded them. But they shall not know it, and thou shalt not declare it to them, nor admonish them, but only record against each individual all the destruction which 65 the shepherds effect each in his time and lay it all before me. 'And I saw till those shepherds pastured in their season, and they began to slay and to destroy more than they were bidden, and they delivered 66 those sheep into the hand of the lions. And the lions and tigers eat and devoured the greater part of those sheep, and the wild boars eat along with them; and they burnt that tower and demolished 67 that house. And I became exceedingly sorrowful over that tower because that house of the sheep was demolished, and afterwards I was unable to see if those sheep entered that house. 68 And the shepherds and their associates delivered over those sheep to all the wild beasts, to devour them, and each one of them received in his time a definite number: it was written by the other 69 in a book how many each one of them destroyed of them. And each one slew and destroyed many 70 more than was prescribed; and I began to weep and lament on account of those sheep. And thus in the vision I saw that one who wrote, how he wrote down every one that was destroyed by those shepherds, day by day, and carried up and laid down and showed actually the whole book to the Lord of the sheep (even) everything that they had done, and all that each one of them had made 71 away with, and all that they had given over to destruction. And the book was read before the Lord of the sheep, and He took the book from his hand and read it and sealed it and laid it down. 72 And forthwith I saw how the shepherds pastured for twelve hours, and behold three of those sheep turned back and came and entered and began to build up all that had fallen down of that 73 house; but the wild boars tried to hinder them, but they were not able. And they began again to build as before, and they reared up that tower, and it was named the high tower; and they began again to place a table before the tower, but all the bread on it was polluted and not pure. 74 And as touching all this the eyes of those sheep were blinded so that they saw not, and (the eyes of) their shepherds likewise; and they delivered them in large numbers to their shepherds for destruction, 15 and they trampled the sheep with their feet and devoured them. And the Lord of the sheep remained unmoved till all the sheep were dispersed over the field and mingled with them (i.e. the 76 beasts), and they (i.e. the shepherds) did not save them out of the hand of the beasts. And this one who wrote the book carried it up, and showed it and read it before the Lord of the sheep, and implored Him on their account, and besought Him on their account as he showed Him all the doings 77 of the shepherds, and gave testimony before Him against all the shepherds. And he took the actual book and laid it down beside Him and departed.

90 1 And I saw till that in this manner thirty-five shepherds undertook the pasturing (of the sheep), and they severally completed their periods as did the first; and others received them into their a 2 hands, to pasture them for their period, each shepherd in his own period. And after that I saw in my vision all the birds of heaven coming, the eagles, the vultures, the kites, the ravens; but the eagles led all the birds; and they began to devour those sheep, and to pick out their eyes and to 3 devour their flesh. And the sheep cried out because their flesh was being devoured by the birds, 4 and as for me I looked and lamented in my sleep over that shepherd who pastured the sheep. And I saw until those sheep were devoured by the dogs and eagles and kites, and they left neither flesh nor skin nor sinew remaining on them till only their bones stood there: and their bones too fell 5 to the earth and the sheep became few. And I saw until that twenty-three had undertaken the pasturing and completed in their several periods fifty-eight times. 6 But behold lambs

were borne by those white sheep, and they began to open their eyes and to see, 7 and to cry to the sheep. Yea, they cried to them, but they did not hearken to what they said to 8 them, but were exceedingly deaf, and their eyes were very exceedingly blinded. And I saw in the vision how the ravens flew upon those lambs and took one of those lambs, and dashed the sheep 9 in pieces and devoured them. And I saw till horns grew upon those lambs, and the ravens cast down their horns; and I saw till there sprouted a great horn of one of those sheep, and their eyes 10 were opened. And it looked at them [and their eyes opened], and it cried to the sheep, and the 11 rams saw it and all ran to it. And notwithstanding all this those eagles and vultures and ravens and kites still kept tearing the sheep and swooping down upon them and devouring them: still the 12 sheep remained silent, but the rams lamented and cried out. And those ravens fought and battled with it and sought to lay low its horn, but they had no power over it. 13 And I saw till the shepherds and eagles and those vultures and kites came, and they cried to the ravens that they should break the horn of that ram, and they battled and fought with it, and it battled with them and cried that its help might come. 19 And I saw till a great sword was given to the sheep, and the sheep proceeded against all the beasts of the field to slay them, and all the beasts and the birds of the heaven fled before their face. 14 And I saw till that man, who wrote down the names of the shepherds [and] carried up into the presence of the Lord of the sheep [came and helped it and showed it everything: he had come down for the help of that ram]. 15 And I saw till the Lord of the sheep came unto them in wrath, and all who saw Him fled, and they all fell into His shadow from before His face. 20 And I saw till a throne was erected in the pleasant land, and the Lord of the sheep sat Himself thereon, and the other took the sealed books and opened those books before the Lord of the sheep. 21 And the Lord called those men the seven first white ones, and commanded that they should bring before Him, beginning with the first star which led the way, all the stars whose privy members and 22 were like those of horses, and they brought them all before Him. And He said to that man who wrote before Him, being one of those seven white ones, and said unto him: 'Take those seventy shepherds to whom I delivered the sheep, and who taking them on their own authority slew more 23 than I commanded them.' And behold they were all bound, I saw, and they all stood before Him. 24 And the judgement was held first over the stars, and they were judged and found guilty, and went to the place of condemnation, and they were cast into an abyss, full of fire and flaming, and full 25 of pillars of fire. And those seventy shepherds were judged and found guilty, and they were cast 26 into that fiery abyss, And I saw at that time how a like abyss was opened in the midst of the earth, full of fire, and they brought those blinded sheep, and they were all judged and found guilty and 27 cast into this fiery abyss, and they burned; now this abyss was to the right of that house. And I saw those sheep burning and their bones burning. 28 And I stood up to see till they folded up that old house; and carried off all the pillars, and all the beams and ornaments of the house were at the same time folded up with it, and they carried 29 it off and laid it in a place in the south of the land. And I saw till the Lord of the sheep brought a new house greater and loftier than that first, and set it up in the place of the first which had been folded up: all its pillars were new, and its ornaments were new and larger than those of the first, the old one which He had taken away, and all the sheep were within it. 30 And I saw all the sheep which had been left, and all the beasts on the earth, and all the birds of the heaven, falling down and doing homage to those sheep and making petition to and obeying 31 them in every thing. And thereafter those three who were clothed in white and had seized me by my hand [who had taken me up before], and the hand of that ram also seizing hold of me, they 32 took me up and set me down in the midst of those sheep before the judgement took place. And those 33 sheep were all white, and their wool was abundant and clean. And all that had been destroyed and dispersed, and all the beasts of the field, and all the birds of the heaven, assembled in that house, and the Lord of the sheep rejoiced with great joy because they were all good and had returned to 34 His house. And I saw till they laid down that sword, which had been given to the sheep, and they brought it back into the house, and it was sealed before the presence of the Lord, and all the sheep 35 were invited into that house, but it held them not. And the eyes of them all were opened, and they 36 saw the good, and there was not one among them that did not see. And I saw that that house was large and broad and very full. 37 And I saw that a white bull was born, with large horns, and all the beasts of the field and all the 38 birds of the air feared him and made petition to him all the time. And I saw till all their generations were transformed, and they all became white bulls; and the first among them became a lamb, and that lamb became a great animal and had great black horns on its head; and the Lord of the sheep 39 rejoiced over it and over all the oxen. And I slept in their midst: and I awoke and saw everything. 40 This is the vision which I saw while I slept, and I awoke and blessed the Lord of righteousness and 41 gave Him glory. Then I wept with a great weeping and my tears stayed not till I could no longer endure it: when I saw, they flowed on account of what I had seen; for everything shall come and 42 be fulfilled, and all the deeds of men in their order were shown to me. On that night I remembered the first dream, and because of it I wept and was troubled because I had seen that vision.

92 1 The book written by Enoch [Enoch indeed wrote this complete doctrine of wisdom, (which is) praised of all men and a judge of all the earth] for all my children who shall dwell on the earth. And for the future generations who shall observe uprightness and peace. 2 Let not your spirit be troubled on account of the times; For the Holy and Great One has appointed days for all things. 3 And the righteous one shall arise from sleep, [Shall arise] and walk in the paths of righteousness, And all his path and conversation shall be in eternal goodness and grace. 4 He will be gracious to the righteous and give him eternal uprightness, And He will give him power so that he shall be (endowed) with goodness and righteousness, And he shall walk in eternal light. 5 And sin shall perish in darkness for ever, And shall no more be seen from that day for evermore.

91 1 'And now, my son Methuselah, call to me all thy brothers And gather together to me all the sons of thy mother; For the word calls me, And the spirit is poured out upon me, That I may show you everything That shall befall you for ever.' 2 And thereupon Methuselah went and summoned to him all his brothers and assembled his relatives. 3 And he spake unto all the children of righteousness and said: 'Hear, ye sons of Enoch, all the words of your father, And hearken aright to the voice of my mouth; For I exhort you and say unto you, beloved: 4 Love uprightness and walk therein. And draw not nigh to uprightness with a double heart, And associate not with those of a double heart, But walk in righteousness, my sons. And it shall guide you on good paths, And righteousness shall be your companion, 5 For I know that violence must increase on the earth, And a great chastisement be executed on the earth, And all unrighteousness come to an end: Yea, it shall be cut off from its roots, And its whole structure be destroyed. 6 And unrighteousness shall again be consummated on the earth, And all the deeds of unrighteousness and of violence And transgression shall prevail in a twofold degree. 7 And when sin and unrighteousness and blasphemy And violence in all kinds of deeds increase, And apostasy and transgression and uncleanness increase, A great chastisement shall come from heaven upon all these, And the holy Lord will come forth with wrath and chastisement To execute judgement on earth. 8 In those days violence shall be cut off from its roots, And the roots of unrighteousness together with deceit, And they shall be destroyed from under heaven. 9 And all the idols of the heathen shall be abandoned, And the temples burned with fire, And they shall remove them from the whole earth, And they (i. e. the heathen) shall be cast into the judgement of fire, And shall perish in wrath and in grievous judgement for ever. 10 And the righteous shall arise from their sleep, And wisdom shall arise and be given unto them. 11 [And after that the roots of unrighteousness shall be cut off, and the sinners shall be destroyed by the sword.. .shall be cut off from the blasphemers in every place, and those who plan violence and those who commit blasphemy shall perish by the sword.] 18 And now I tell you, my sons, and show you The paths of righteousness and the paths of violence. Yea, I will show them to you again That ye may know what will come to pass. 19 And now, hearken unto me, my sons, And walk in the paths of righteousness, And walk not in the paths of violence; For all who walk in the paths of unrighteousness shall perish for ever.'

93 1, 2 And after that Enoch both gave and began to recount from the books. And Enoch said: 'Concerning the children of righteousness and concerning the elect of the world, And concerning the plant of uprightness, I will speak these things, Yea, I Enoch will declare (them) unto you, my sons: According to that which appeared to me in the heavenly vision, And which I have known through the word of the holy angels, And have learnt from the heavenly tablets.' 3 And Enoch began to recount from the books and said: 'I was born the seventh in the first week, While judgement and righteousness still endured. 4 And after me there shall arise in the second week great wickedness, And deceit shall have sprung up; And in it there shall be the first end. And in it a man shall be saved; And after it is ended unrighteousness shall grow up, And a law shall be made for the sinners. 5 And after that in the third week at its close A man shall be elected as the plant of righteous judgement, And his posterity shall become the plant of righteousness for evermore. 6 And after that in the fourth week, at its close, Visions of the holy and righteous shall be seen, And a law for all generations and an enclosure shall be made for them. 7 And after that in the fifth week, at its close, The house of glory and dominion shall be built for ever. 8 And after that in the sixth week all who live in it shall be blinded, And the hearts of all of them shall godlessly forsake wisdom. And in it a man shall ascend; And at its close the house of dominion shall be burnt with fire, And the whole race of the chosen root shall be dispersed. And after that in the seventh week shall an apostate generation arise, And many shall be its deeds, And all its deeds shall be apostate. 10 And at its close shall be elected The elect righteous of the eternal, plant of righteousness, To receive sevenfold instruction concerning all His creation. 11 [For who is there of all the children of men that is able to hear the voice of the Holy One without being troubled? And who can think His thoughts? and who is there that can behold all the works 12 of heaven? And how should there be one who could behold the heaven, and who is there that could understand the things of heaven and see a soul or a spirit and could tell thereof, or ascend and see 13 all their ends and think them or do like them? And who is there of all men that could know what is the breadth and the length of the earth, and to whom has been shown the measure of all of them? 14 Or is there any one who could discern the length of the heaven and how great is its height, and upon what it is founded, and how great is the number of the stars, and where all the luminaries rest?]

91 12 And after that there shall be another, the eighth week, that of righteousness, And a sword shall be given to it that a righteous judgement may be executed on the oppressors, And sinners shall be delivered into the hands of the righteous. 13 And at its close they shall acquire houses through their righteousness, And a house shall be built for the Great King in glory for evermore, 14d And all mankind shall look to the path of uprightness. 14a And after that, in the ninth week, the righteous judgement shall be revealed to the whole world, b And all the works of the godless shall vanish from all the earth, c And the world shall be written down for destruction. 15 And after this, in the tenth week in the seventh part, There shall be the great eternal judgement, In which He will execute vengeance amongst the angels. 16 And the first heaven shall depart and pass away, And a new heaven shall appear, And all the powers of the heavens shall give sevenfold light. 17 And after that there will be many weeks without number for ever, And all shall be in goodness and righteousness, And sin shall no more be mentioned for ever.

94 1 And now I say unto you, my sons, love righteousness and walk therein; For the paths of righteousness are worthy of acceptation, But the paths of unrighteousness shall suddenly be destroyed and vanish. 2 And to certain men of a generation shall the paths of violence and of death be revealed, And they shall hold themselves afar from them, And shall not follow them. 3 And now I say unto you the righteous: Walk not in the paths of wickedness, nor in the paths of death, And draw not nigh to them, lest ye be destroyed. 4 But seek and choose for yourselves righteousness and an elect life, And walk in the paths of peace, And ye shall live and prosper. 5 And hold fast my words in the thoughts of your hearts, And suffer them not to be effaced from your hearts; For I know that sinners will tempt men to evilly entreat wisdom, So that no place may be found for her, And no manner of temptation may minish. 6 Woe to those who build unrighteousness and oppression And lay deceit as a foundation; For they shall be suddenly overthrown, And they shall have no peace. 7 Woe to those who build their houses with sin; For from all their foundations shall they be overthrown, And by the sword shall they fall. [And those who acquire gold and silver in judgement suddenly shall perish.] 8 Woe to you, ye rich, for ye have trusted in your riches, And from your riches shall ye depart, Because ye have not remembered the Most High in the days of your riches. 9 Ye have committed blasphemy and unrighteousness, And have become ready for the day of slaughter, And the day of darkness and the day of the great judgement. 10 Thus I speak and declare unto you: He who hath created you will overthrow you, And for your fall there shall be no compassion, And your Creator will rejoice at your destruction. 11 And your righteous ones in those days shall be A reproach to the sinners and the godless.

95 1 Oh that mine eyes were [a cloud of] waters That I might weep over you, And pour down my tears as a cloud of waters: That so I might rest from my trouble of heart! 2 Who has permitted you to practice reproaches and wickedness? And so judgement shall overtake you, sinners. 3 Fear not the sinners, ye righteous; For again will the Lord deliver them into your hands, That ye may execute judgement upon them according to your desires. 4 Woe to you who fulminate

anathemas which cannot be reversed: Healing shall therefore be far from you because of your sins. 5 Woe to you who requite your neighbour with evil; For ye shall be requited according to your works. 6 Woe to you, lying witnesses, And to those who weigh out injustice, For suddenly shall ye perish. 7 Woe to you, sinners, for ye persecute the righteous; For ye shall be delivered up and persecuted because of injustice, And heavy shall its yoke be upon you.

96 1 Be hopeful, ye righteous; for suddenly shall the sinners perish before you, And ye shall have lordship over them according to your desires. 2 [And in the day of the tribulation of the sinners, Your children shall mount and rise as eagles, And higher than the vultures will be your nest, And ye shall ascend and enter the crevices of the earth, And the clefts of the rock for ever as coneys before the unrighteous, And the sirens shall sigh because of you and weep.] 3 Wherefore fear not, ye that have suffered; For healing shall be your portion, And a bright light shall enlighten you, And the voice of rest ye shall hear from heaven. 4 Woe unto you, ye sinners, for your riches make you appear like the righteous, But your hearts convict you of being sinners, And this fact shall be a testimony against you for a memorial of (your) evil deeds. 5 Woe to you who devour the finest of the wheat, And drink wine in large bowls, And tread under foot the lowly with your might. 6 Woe to you who drink water from every fountain, For suddenly shall ye be consumed and wither away, Because ye have forsaken the fountain of life. 7 Woe to you who work unrighteousness And deceit and blasphemy: It shall be a memorial against you for evil. 8 Woe to you, ye mighty, Who with might oppress the righteous; For the day of your destruction is coming. In those days many and good days shall come to the righteous -- in the day of your judgement.

97 1 Believe, ye righteous, that the sinners will become a shame And perish in the day of unrighteousness. 2 Be it known unto you (ye sinners) that the Most High is mindful of your destruction, And the angels of heaven rejoice over your destruction. 3 What will ye do, ye sinners, And whither will ye flee on that day of judgement, When ye hear the voice of the prayer of the righteous? 4 Yea? ye shall fare like unto them, Against whom this word shall be a testimony: "Ye have been companions of sinners." 5 And in those days the prayer of the righteous shall reach unto the Lord, And for you the days of your judgement shall come. 6 And all the words of your unrighteousness shall be read out before the Great Holy One, And your faces shall be covered with shame, And He will reject every work which is grounded on unrighteousness. 7 Woe to you, ye sinners, who live on the mid ocean and on the dry land, Whose remembrance is evil against you. 8 Woe to you who acquire silver and gold in unrighteousness and say: "We have become rich with riches and have possessions; And have acquired everything we have desired. 9 And now let us do what we purposed: For we have gathered silver, 9c And many are the husbandmen in our houses." 9d And our granaries are (brim) full as with water; 10 Yea and like water your lies shall flow away; For your riches shall not abide But speedily ascend from you; For ye have acquired it all in unrighteousness, And ye shall be given over to a great curse.

98 1 And now I swear unto you, to the wise and to the foolish, For ye shall have manifold experiences on the earth. 2 For ye men shall put on more adornments than a woman, And coloured garments more than a virgin: In royalty and in grandeur and in power, And in silver and in gold and in purple, And in splendour and in food they shall be poured out as water. 3 Therefore they shall be wanting in doctrine and wisdom, And they shall perish thereby together with their possessions; And with all their glory and their splendour, And in shame and in slaughter and in great destitution, Their spirits shall be cast into the furnace of fire. 4 I have sworn unto you, ye sinners, as a mountain has not become a slave, And a hill does not become the handmaid of a woman, Even so sin has not been sent upon the earth, But man of himself has created it, And under a great curse shall they fall who commit it. 5 And barrenness has not been given to the woman, But on account of the deeds of her own hands she dies without children. 6 I have sworn unto you, ye sinners, by the Holy Great One, That all your evil deeds are revealed in the heavens, And that none of your deeds of oppression are covered and hidden. 7 And do not think in your spirit nor say in your heart that ye do not know and that ye do not see 8 that every sin is every day recorded in heaven in the presence of the Most High. From henceforth ye know that all your oppression wherewith ye oppress is written down every day till the day of your judgement. 9 Woe to you, ye fools, for through your folly shall ye perish: and ye transgress against thw wise, 10 and so good hap shall not be your portion. And now, know ye that ye are prepared for the day of destruction: wherefore do not hope to live, ye sinners, but ye shall depart and die; for ye know no ransom; for ye are prepared for the day of the great judgement, for the day of tribulation and great shame for your spirits. 11 Woe to you, ye obstinate of heart, who work wickedness and eat blood: Whence have ye good things to eat and to drink and to be filled? From all the good things which the Lord the Mast High has placed in abundance on the earth; therefore ye shall have no peace. 12 Woe to you who love the deeds of unrighteousness: wherefore do ye hope for good hap unto yourselves? know that ye shall be delivered into the hands of the righteous, and they shall cut 13 off your necks and slay you, and have no mercy upon you. Woe to you who rejoice in the tribulation 14 of the righteous; for no grave shall be dug for you. Woe to you who set at nought the words of 15 the righteous; for ye shall have no hope of life. Woe to you who write down lying and godless words; for they write down their lies that men may hear them and act godlessly towards (their) 16 neighbour. Therefore they shall have no peace but die a sudden death.

99 1 Woe to you who work godlessness, And glory in lying and extol them: Ye shall perish, and no happy life shall be yours. 2 Woe to them who pervert the words of uprightness, And transgress the eternal law, And transform themselves into what they were not [into sinners]: They shall be trodden under foot upon the earth. 3 In those days make ready, ye righteous, to raise your prayers as a memorial, And place them as a testimony before the angels, That they may place the sin of the sinners for a memorial before the Most High. 4 In those days the nations shall be stirred up, And the families of the nations shall arise on the day of destruction. 5 And in those days the destitute shall go forth and carry off their children, And they shall abandon them, so that their children shall perish through them: Yea, they shall abandon their children (that are still) sucklings, and not return to them, And shall have no pity on their beloved ones. 6,7 And again I swear to you, ye sinners, that sin is prepared for a day of unceasing bloodshed. And they who worship stones, and grave images of gold and silver and wood (and stone) and clay, and those who worship impure spirits and demons, and all kinds of idols not according to knowledge, shall get no manner of help from them. 8 And they shall become godless by reason of the folly of their hearts, And their eyes shall be blinded through the fear of their hearts And through visions in their dreams. 9 Through these they shall become godless and fearful; For they shall have wrought all their work in a lie, And shall have worshipped a stone: Therefore in an instant shall they perish. 10 But in those days blessed are all they who accept the words of wisdom, and understand them, And observe the paths of the Most High, and walk in the path of His righteousness, And become not godless with the godless; For they shall be saved. 11 Woe to you who spread evil to your neighbours; For you shall be slain in Sheol. 12 Woe to you who make deceitful and false measures, And (to them) who cause bitterness on the earth; For they shall thereby be utterly consumed. 13 Woe to you who build your houses through the grievous toil of others, And all their building materials are the bricks and stones of sin; I tell you ye shall have no peace. 14 Woe to them who reject the measure and eternal heritage of their fathers And whose souls follow after idols; For they shall have no rest. 15 Woe to them who work unrighteousness and help oppression, And slay their neighbours until the day of the great judgement. 16 For He shall cast down your glory, And bring affliction on your hearts, And shall arouse His fierce indignation And destroy you all with the sword; And all the holy and righteous shall remember your sins.

100 1 And in those days in one place the fathers together with their sons shall be smitten And brothers one with another shall fall in death Till the streams flow with their blood. 2 For a man shall not withhold his hand from slaying his sons and his sons' sons, And the sinner shall not withhold his hand from his honoured brother: From dawn till sunset they shall slay one another. 3 And the horse shall walk up to the breast in the blood of sinners, And the chariot shall be submerged to its height. 4 In those days the angels shall descend into the secret places And gather together into one place all those who brought down sin, And the Most High will arise on that day of judgement To execute great judgement amongst sinners. 5 And over all the righteous and holy He will appoint guardians from amongst the holy angels To guard them as the apple of an eye, Until He makes an end of all wickedness and all sin, And though the righteous sleep a long sleep, they have nought to fear. 6 And (then) the children of the earth shall see the wise in security. And shall understand all the words of this book, And recognize that their riches shall not be able to save them In the overthrow of their sins. 7 Woe to you, Sinners, on the day of strong anguish, Ye who afflict the righteous and burn them with fire: Ye shall be requited according to your works. 8 Woe to you, ye obstinate of heart, Who watch in order to devise wickedness: Therefore shall fear come upon you And there shall be none to help you. 9 Woe to you, ye sinners, on account of the words of your mouth, And on account of the deeds of your hands which your godlessness has wrought, In blazing flames burning worse than fire shall ye burn. 10 And now, know ye that from the angels He will inquire as to your deeds in heaven, from the sun and from the moon and from the stars in reference to your sins because upon the earth ye execute 11 judgement on the righteous. And He will summon to testify against you every cloud and mist and dew and rain; for they shall all be withheld because of you from descending upon you, and they 12 shall be mindful of your sins. And now give presents to the ram that it be not withheld from descending upon you, nor yet the dew, when it has received gold and silver from you that it may descend. 13 When the hoar-frost and snow with their chilliness, and all the snow-storms with all their plagues fall upon you, in those days ye shall not be able to stand before them.

101 1 Observe the heaven, ye children of heaven, and every work of the Most High, and fear ye Him and work 2 no evil in His presence. If He closes the windows of heaven, and withholds the rain and 3 the dew from descending on the earth on your account, what will ye do then? And if He sends His anger upon you because of your deeds, ye cannot petition Him; for ye spake proud and insolent 4 words against His righteousness: therefore ye shall have no peace. And see ye not the sailors of the ships, how their ships are tossed to and fro by the waves, and are shaken by the winds, and are 5 in sore trouble ? And therefore do they fear because all their goodly possessions go upon the sea with them, and they have evil forebodings of heart that the sea will swallow them and they will 6 perish therein. Are not the entire sea and all its waters, and all its movements, the work of the Most 7 High, and has He not set limits to its doings, and confined it throughout by the sand? And at His reproof it is afraid and dries up, and all its fish die and all that is in it; but ye sinners that are 8 on the earth fear Him not. Has He not made the heaven and the earth, and all that is therein Who has given understanding and wisdom to everything that moves on the earth and in the sea? 9 Do not the sailors of the ships fear the sea? Yet sinners fear not the Most High.

102 1 In those days when He hath brought a grievous fire upon you, Whither will ye flee, and where will ye find deliverance? And when He launches forth His word against you Will you not be affrighted and fear? 2 And all the luminaries shall be affrighted with great fear, And all the earth shall be affrighted and tremble and be alarmed. 3 And all the angels shall execute their commands And shall seek to hide themselves from the presence of the Great Glory, And the children of earth shall tremble and quake; And ye sinners shall be cursed for ever, And ye shall have no peace. 4 Fear ye not, ye souls of the righteous, And be hopeful ye that have died in righteousness. 5 And grieve not if your soul into Sheol has descended in grief, And that in your life your body fared not according to your goodness, But wait for the day of the judgement of sinners And for the day of cursing and chastisement. 6 And yet when ye die the sinners speak over you: "As we die, so die the righteous, And what benefit do they reap for their deeds? 7 Behold, even as we, so do they die in grief and darkness, And what have they more than we? From henceforth we are equal. 8 And what will they receive and what will they see for ever? Behold, they too have died, And henceforth for ever shall they see no light." 9 I tell you, ye sinners, ye are content to eat and drink, and rob and sin, and strip men naked, and 10 acquire wealth and see good days. Have ye seen the righteous how their end falls out, that no manner 11 of violence is found in them till their death? "Nevertheless they perished and became as though they had not been, and their spirits descended into Sheol in tribulation."

103 1 Now, therefore, I swear to you, the righteous, by the glory of the Great and Honoured and 2 Mighty One in dominion, and by His greatness I swear to you. I know a mystery And have read the heavenly tablets, And have seen the holy books, And have found written therein and inscribed regarding them: 3 That all goodness and joy and glory are prepared for them, And written down for the spirits of those who have died in righteousness, And that manifold good shall be given to you in recompense for your labours, And that your lot is abundantly beyond the lot of the living. 4 And the spirits of you who have died in righteousness shall live and rejoice, And their spirits shall not perish, nor their memorial from before the face of the Great One Unto all the generations of the world: wherefore no longer fear their contumely. 5 Woe to you, ye sinners, when ye have died, If ye die in the wealth of your sins, And those who are like you say regarding you: "Blessed are the sinners: they have seen all their days. 6 And now they have died in prosperity and in wealth, And have not seen tribulation or murder in their life; And they have died in honour, And judgement has not been executed on them during their life." 7 Know ye, that their souls will be made to descend into Sheol And they shall be wretched in their great tribulation. 8 And into darkness and chains and aburning flame where there is grievous judgement shall your spirits enter; And the great judgement shall be for all the generations of the world. Woe to you, for ye shall have no peace. 9 Say not in regard to the righteous and good who are in life: "In our troubled days we have toiled laboriously and experienced every trouble, And met with much evil and been consumed, 10 And we have been destroyed and have not found any to help us even with a word: 11 We have been tortured [and destroyed], and not hoped to see life from day to day. We hoped to be the head and have become the tail: We have toiled laboriously and had no satisfaction in our toil; And we have become the food of the sinners and the unrighteous, And they have laid their yoke heavily upon us. 12 They have had dominion over us that hated us and smote us; And to those that hated us we have bowed our necks But they pitied us not. 13 We desired to get away from them that we might escape and be at rest, But found no place whereunto we should flee and be safe from them. 14 And we complained to the rulers in our tribulation, And cried out against those who devoured us, But they did not attend to our cries And would not hearken to our voice. 15 And they helped those who robbed us and devoured us and those who made us few; and they concealed their oppression, and they did not remove from us the yoke of those that devoured us and dispersed us and murdered us, and they concealed their murder, and remembered not that they had lifted up their hands against us.

104 1 I swear unto you, that in heaven the angels remember you for good before the glory of the Great 2 One: and your names are written before the glory of the Great One. Be hopeful; for aforetime ye were put to shame through ill and affliction; but now ye shall shine as the lights of heaven, 3 ye shall shine and ye shall be seen, and the portals of heaven shall be opened to you. And in your cry, cry for judgement, and it shall appear to you; for all your tribulation shall be visited on the 4 rulers, and on all who helped those who plundered you. Be hopeful, and cast not away your hope; 5 for ye shall have great joy as the angels of heaven. What shall ye be obliged to do ? Ye shall not have to hide on the day of the great judgement and ye shall not be found as sinners, and the eternal 6 judgement shall be far from you for all the generations of the world. And now fear not, ye righteous, when ye see the sinners growing strong and prospering in their ways: be not companions with them, 7 but keep afar from their violence; for ye shall become companions of the hosts of heaven. And, although ye sinners say: "All our sins shall not be searched out and be written down," nevertheless 8 they shall write down all your sins every day. And now I show unto you that light and darkness, 9 day and night, see all your sins. Be not godless in your hearts, and lie not and alter not the words of uprightness, nor charge with lying the words of the Holy Great One, nor take account of your 10 idols; for all your lying and all your godlessness issue not in righteousness but in great sin. And now I know this mystery, that sinners will alter and pervert the words of righteousness in many ways, and will speak wicked words, and lie, and practice great deceits, and write books concerning 11 their words. But when they write down truthfully all my words in their languages, and do not change or minish ought from my words but write them all down truthfully all that I first testified 12 concerning them. Then, I know another mystery, that books will be given to the righteous and the 13 wise to become a cause of joy and uprightness and much wisdom. And to them shall the books be given, and they shall believe in them and rejoice over them, and then shall all the righteous who have learnt therefrom all the paths of uprightness be recompensed.'

105 1 In those days the Lord bade (them) to summon and testify to the children of earth concerning their wisdom: Show (it) unto them; for ye are their guides, and a recompense over the whole earth. 2 For I and My Son will be united with them for ever in the paths of uprightness in their lives; and ye shall have peace: rejoice, ye children of uprightness. Amen.

FRAGMENT OF THE BOOK OF NOAH

106 1 And after some days my son Methuselah took a wife for his son Lamech, and she became 2 pregnant by him and bore a son. And his body was white as snow and red as the blooming of a rose, and the hair of his head and his long locks were white as wool, and his eyes beautiful And when he opened his eyes, he lighted up the whole house like the sun, and the whole house 3 was very bright. And thereupon he arose in the hands of the midwife, opened his mouth, and conversed with the Lord of righteousness. 4 And his father Lamech was afraid of him and 5 fled, and came to his father Methuselah. And he said unto him: 'I have begotten a strange son, diverse from and unlike man, and resembling the sons of the God of heaven; and his nature is different and he is not like us, and his eyes are as the rays of the sun, and his countenance 6 is glorious. And it seems to me that he is not sprung from me but from the angels, and I fear that in his days a wonder may be 7 wrought on the earth. And now, my father, I am here to petition thee and implore thee that thou mayst go to Enoch, our father, and learn from him the truth, for his dwelling-place is 8 amongst the angels.' And when Methuselah heard the words of his son, he came to me to the ends of the earth; for he had heard that I was there, and he cried aloud, and I heard his voice and I came to him. And I said unto him: 'Behold, here am I, my son, wherefore hast 9 thou come to me? 'And he answered and said: 'Because of a great cause of anxiety have I come to thee, and because of a disturbing vision 10 have I approached. And now, my father, hear me: unto Lamech my son there hath been born a son, the like of whom there is none, and his nature is not lkie man's nature, and the colour of his body is whiter than snow and redder than the bloom of a rose, and the hair of his head is whiter than white wool, and his eyes are like the rays of the sun, and he opened his eyes and 11 thereupon lighted up the whole house. And he arose in the hands of the midwife, and opened 12 his mouth and blessed the Lord of heaven. And his father Lamech became afraid and fled to me, and did not believe that he was sprung from him, but that he was in the likeness of the angels of heaven; and behold I have come to thee that thou mayst make known to me the truth. 13 And I, Enoch, answered and said unto him: 'The Lord will do a new thing on the earth, and this I have already seen in a vision, and make known to thee that in the generation of my father Jared some of the angels of heaven 14 transgressed the word of the Lord. And behold they commit sin and transgress the law, and have united themselves with women and commit sin with them, and have married some of them, 17 and have begot children by them. And they shall produce on the earth giants not according to the spirit, but according to the flesh, and there shall be a great punishment on the earth, and the 15 earth shall be cleansed from all impurity. Yea, there shall come a great destruction over the whole earth, and there shall be a deluge and 16 a great destruction for one year. And this son who has been born unto you shall be left on the earth, and his three children shall be saved with him: when all mankind that are on the earth 18 shall die [he and his sons shall be saved]. And now make known to thy son Lamech that he who has been born is in truth his son, and call his name Noah; for he shall be left to you, and he and his sons shall be saved from the destruction, which shall come upon the earth on account of all the sin and all the unrighteousness, which shall be consummated on the earth in his days. 19 And after that there shall be still more unrighteousness than that which was first consummated on the earth; for I know the mysteries of the holy ones; for He, the Lord, has showed me and informed me, and I have read (them) in the heavenly tablets.

107 1 And I saw written on them that generation upon generation shall transgress, till a generation of righteousness arises, and transgression is destroyed and sin passes away from the earth, and all 2 manner of good comes upon it. And now, my son, go and make known to thy son Lamech that this 3 son, which has been born, is in truth his son, and that (this) is no lie.' And when Methuselah had heard the words of his father Enoch -- for he had shown to him everything in secret he returned and showed (them) to him and called the name of that son Noah; for he will comfort the earth after all the destruction.

108 1 Another book which Enoch wrote for his son Methuselah and for those who will come after him, 2 and keep the law in the last days. Ye who have done good shall wait for those days till an end is 3 made of those who work evil, and an end of the might of the transgressors. And wait ye indeed till sin has passed away, for their names shall be blotted out of the book of life and out of the holy books, and their seed shall be destroyed for ever, and their spirits shall be slain, and they shall cry and make lamentation in a place that is a chaotic wilderness, and in the fire shall they 4 burn; for there is no earth there. And I saw there something like an invisible cloud; for by reason of its depth I could not look over, and I saw a flame of fire blazing brightly, and things like shining 5 mountains circling and sweeping to and fro. And I asked one of the Holy angels who was with me and said unto him: 'What is this shining thing? for it is not a heaven but only the flame of a blazing 6 fire, and the voice of weeping and crying and lamentation and strong pain.' And he said unto me: 'This place which thou seest -- here are cast the spirits of sinners and blasphemers, and of those who work wickedness, and of those who pervert everything that the Lord hath spoken through the mouth 7 of the prophets. (even) the things that shall be. For some of them are written and inscribed above in the heaven, in order that the angels may read them and know that which shall befall the sinners, and the spirits of the humble, and of those who have afflicted their bodies, and been recompensed 8 by God; and of those who have been put to shame by wicked men. Who love God and loved neither gold nor silver nor any of the good things which are in the world, but gave over their bodies to 9 torture. Who, since they came into being, longed not after earthly food, but regarded everything as a passing breath, and lived accordingly, and the Lord tried them much, and their spirits were 10 found pure so that they should bless His name. And all the blessings destined for them I have recounted in the books. And He hath assigned them their recompense, because they have been found to be such as loved heaven more than their life in the world, and though they were trodden under foot of wicked men, and experienced abuse and reviling from them and were put to shame, 11 yet they blessed Me. And now I will summon the spirits of the good who belong to the generation of light, and I will transform those who were born in darkness, who in the flesh were not recompensed 12 with such honour as their faithfulness deserved. And I will bring forth in shining light those who 13 have loved My holy name, and I will seat each on the throne of his honour. And they shall be resplendent for times without number; for righteousness is the judgement of God; for to the faithful 14 He will give faithfulness in the habitation of .upright paths. And they shall see those who were 15 born in darkness led into darkness, while the righteous shall be resplendent. And the sinners shall cry aloud and see them resplendent, and they indeed will go where days and seasons are prescribed for them.'

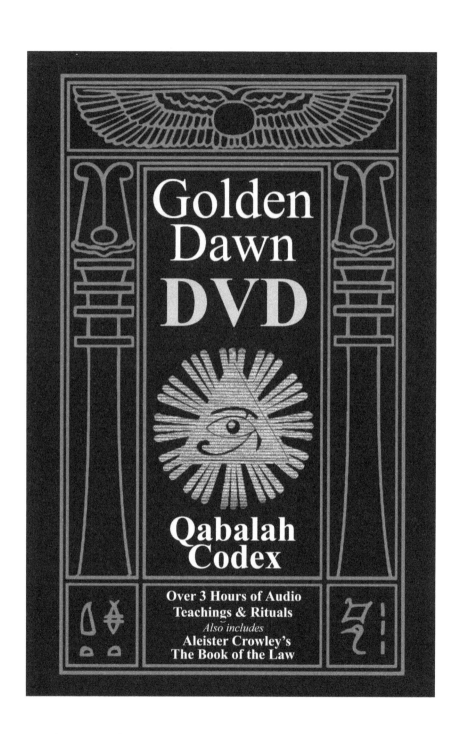

Available from www.glastonburybooks.com

THE GOLDEN DAWN QABALAH CODEX DVD

The Collected Qabalah
Audio teachings of Steven Ashe

Contents:

The Qabalah and the Magical Tradition, The philosophy of Magick and Mysticism, Self Development and Occult practices, Initiation and the Qabalah, The Sephiroth Belimah - Voices from Nothing , Macrocosm and Microcosm Gemetria & the sacred alphabet, The Angels of the Schemhamphorash , History of the Literary Qabalah, The Sephiroth upon the Tree of Life, Malkuth and Daath: The Fall, The Four worlds of the Qabalist, The Rite of the Pentagram , The Qabalah of 50 Gates , The Three orders of Being, Psycho-Static; Psycho-Kinetic; Psycho-Telios
Aleister Crowley's The Book of the Law (full length audio)
Methods of Invocation
The Binding of the Qlipoth
The Grand Qabalistic Invocation
Consecration the Water, Salt & Ash
The Seven Great Planetary Invocations
7 Lectures on Advanced Qabalah
& the experience of the Astral Sephiroth

Plus 6 Full length e-Books
Complete Rituals of the Golden Dawn (355pages)
The Enochian Magic of the Golden Dawn (105 pages)
The Qabalah Codex (188 Pages - including the text of the ritual invocations above)
The Hermetic Qabalah of Anna Kingsford
The Key of Solomon (including seals & talismans)
The Book of Enoch (The Book of the Watchers) - 1st Century BC text of Qabalah tradition dealing with the lore of the fallen angels.

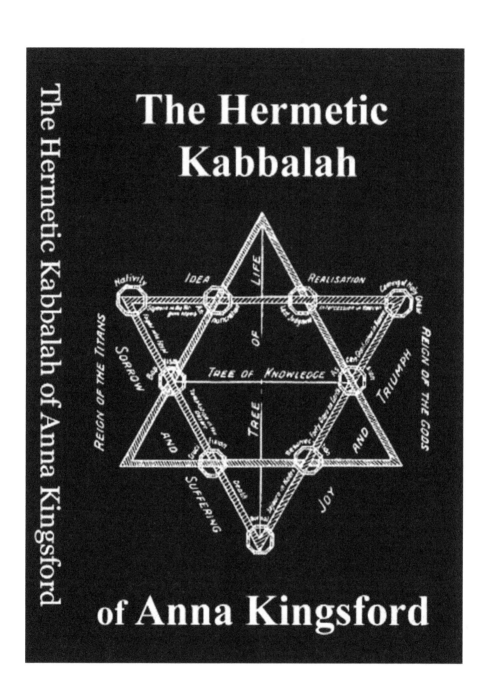

The Hermetic Kabbalah of Anna Kingsford

The Hermetic Kabbalah of Anna Kingsford, The Credo of Christendom & other addresses and essays on Esoteric Christianity, by Anna Kingsford and Edward Maitland represented for the 21st century enquirer. In 1883 Anna Kingsford was made President of the Theosophical Society, promoted a Western, Christian and Hermetic Esotericism. She claimed to recieve mystical insights in trance states and sleep, she was an advocate of women's rights anti-vivisection & vegetarianism. Mahatma Gandhi is said to have sold her books.

The Hermetic Kabbalah of Anna Kingsford

ISBN: 978-1-84753-313-5

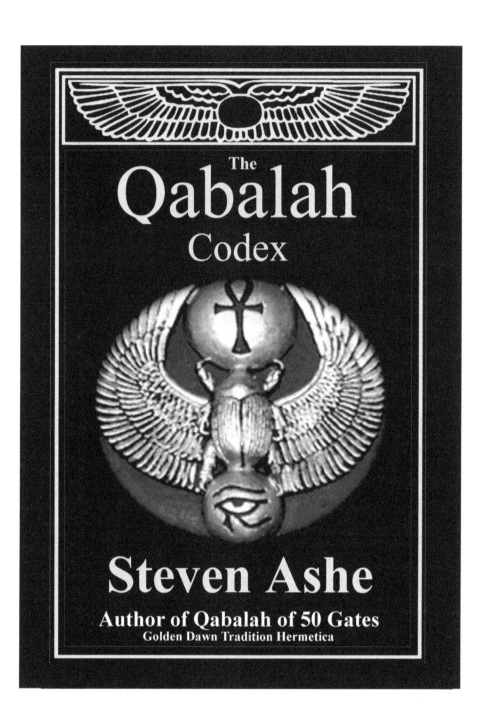

Available from www.glastonburybooks.com

The Qabalah Codex
by Steven Ashe

Containing teachings on the fundamentals of Qabalistic theory, an initiated commentary upon the Tarot and Qabalistic symbolism, the official planetary & zodiacal invocations of the Golden Dawn lodge of the FSR, Zodiacal Magic, the planetary and zodiacal significance of the 72 Angels of the Shemhamphorash (Divided Name), essential esoteric rites for the Opening of the Temple, the Sidereal Zodiac and the employment of the Angels with relevance to the fixed-stars, etc. From the author of Qabalah of 50 Gates and The Complete Golden Dawn Initiate.

The Qabalah Codex
ISBN: 978-1-84753-730-0
Glastonbury Books
www.glastonburybooks.com

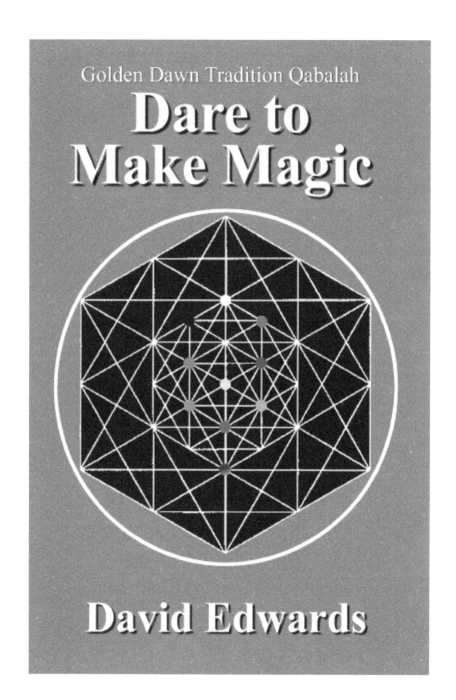

Golden Dawn Tradition Qabalah

Dare to
Make Magic

David Edwards

Available from www.glastonburybooks.com

Golden Dawn Tradition Qabalah Dare to Make Magic

Dare to Make Magic was originally made available as an Order of the Cubic Stone publication. The publication of David Edwards' Dare to Make Magic provides a pathway for serious students of the occult arts. This Glastonbury Books edition includes an expansion of the original book with additions consisting of an extract from personal magical diaries, examples of short ceremonies and meditational rituals. The latter are generally in line with the magical paradigm know to initiates as the Annals of Time and Space.

David Edwards was a founder member and Warden of the Order of the Cubic Stone (1960), an esoteric study group pursuing the evolved tradition of the Golden Dawn tradition of Western Hermetics & Qabalah. The teachings contained within Dare to Make Magic are illustrative of the highly qualitative and practical approach which characterised the OCS as the teaching group 'par excellance' of the Western Estoeric tradition during the late 20th Century.

Golden Dawn Tradition Qabalah
Dare to Make Magic
ISBN 978-0-9556931-2-0
Glastonbury Books
www.glastonburybooks.com

CPSIA information can be obtained
at www.ICGtesting.com
Printed in the USA
BVHW031832200120
569988BV00004B/12